James Miller

1860-1947

I intend this publication as a personal tribute to my father, the Scottish architect James Miller, RSA FRIBA FRIAS. The selection of photographs and illustrations has been compiled to reflect the many styles and types of buildings produced by his Glasgow practice during a career which spanned almost 60 years, with the assistance of three brilliant draughtsmen, Mr Gunn, Mr Walker and Mr Manson. The publication contains a wealth of information about the changes in Scottish architecture during these years, and I am grateful to James Rennie of Frank Burnet Bell & Partners whose gift of their collection of my father's drawings to the RIAS began the whole thing.

Mabel Harper

Acknowledgements

Arthur Bryce, Perth & Kinross District Library; Roger Bainbridge; Carnegie Library, Reference Dept, Ayr; Eleanor Cordiner, RSAC Glasgow; Mike Davis of AHSS; J Carrick; staff at Clydebank Library; Alexander Dunlop; staff at the Mitchell Library; Edinburgh Central Library; Ian Fraser; North Glasgow College, Springburn; Glasgow School of Art Library; Ian Gow and staff at the RCAHMS; John Hannay; Mrs Mabel Harper; John Hume; Keith Hunter, architectural photographer; Institution of Civil Engineers, London; Kyle and Carrick District Council; Scott Lee, architectural photographer; G D Lodge Architects; David Hanley of I H McKinney Architects; High Commission of India, London; Mrs McConnell; Charles McKean and staff at RIAS; Neil McLeod, University of Strathclyde; Anne O'Connor; John Paton; Peebles Hydro Hotel; Perth & Kinross Library; ScotRail; Scottish Records Office; Elizabeth Sloan, for hours of patient typing; staff at Stirling Library; Sam Small; Eleanor Smart; Roger Strugnell; staff at Strathclyde Regional Archives; Jane Thomas; Head Teacher, Troon Primary School; Turnberry Hotel; Dr David Walker; Professor Frank Walker; Vera Watson.

Some of the buildings described are either open to the public or visible from the road. Some, however, are privately owned and readers are asked to respect the occupiers' privacy.

Consultant: David Walker
Editor: Charles McKean
Editorial consultant: Win Elliott

Royal Incorporation of Architects in Scotland
ISBN 1 873190 15 8
First published 1993

Cover illustrations: James Miller, Architect (*top*)
Canniesburn Hospital, Glasgow (*left*)
Commercial Bank of Scotland, West Nile Street, Glasgow (*right*)

Typesetting, page make-up and picture scans: Almond Design, Edinburgh
Printed by Butler & Tanner, Frome, Somerset

Contents

Introduction and critical analysis	**i-7**
1888-1900	**8-17**
1901-14	**18-35**
1915-29	**36-47**
1930-38	**48-56**
Notes & Bibliography	**57**
Chronology	**58-9**
Index	**60**
Illustration Credits	**Inside back cover**

James Miller Introduction

1

James Miller was born in 1860 at Auchtergaven, Perthshire, and spent his childhood at Cairnie, Forteviot. A farmer's son, he was educated at Perth Academy, then took up an apprenticeship with the Perth architect Andrew Heiton, a contemporary of Philip Webb, and former employee of Norman Shaw in London. Heiton was also closely associated with the Scottish railway companies. Such English Arts & Crafts connections were to prove very influential to Miller's early houses, churches and railway stations. On completing his apprenticeship, Miller worked in Edinburgh in the office of Hippolyte J Blanc, before moving, in 1888, to join the drawing office of the Caledonian Railway Company in Glasgow. He finally set up practice on his own account in 1893.

Glasgow was then at its apogee as the Second City of the Empire. Between 1870 and 1880 the tonnage of vessels arriving up the Clyde had increased by 230%, and in 1878 the city had embarked on one of its greatest feats of engineering the creation of great shipping docks. The city had enjoyed great affinity with the eastern seaboard of America ever since the development of the lucrative tobacco trade with Virginia from c.1720; and, by the mid 18th century, it was already displaying the influence of architectural developments in eastern America and vice-versa. It was a thoroughly modern metropolis.

Glasgow in the 1890s was unusually stimulating. In 1896 J J Burnet visited the United States and forged a friendship with McKim and Stanford White – at a time when McKim, Mead and White were transforming the architecture of America, along with H H Richardson, Adler and Sullivan, Burnham and Root, and Holabird and Roche. The

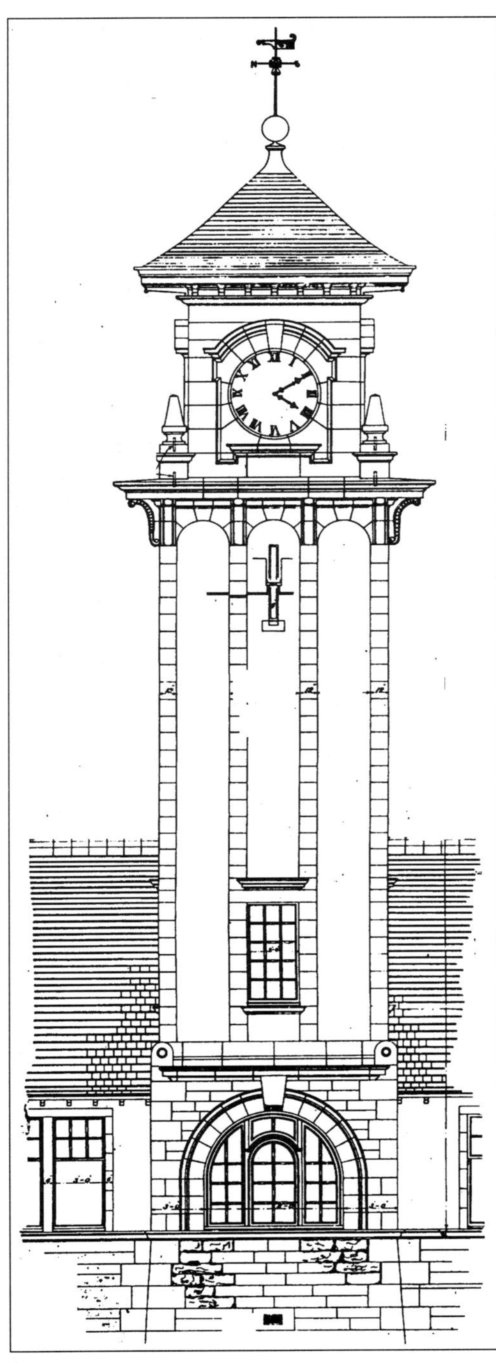

2

1 - Elevation detail, Caledonian Mansions, Great Western Road, Glasgow

2 - Wemyss Bay Railway Station Clock Tower

Working closely with civil engineers provided Miller with an understanding of, if not fondness for, engineering and its approach to solving problems. He was a simple, rigorous man whose designs were always well honed and scrupulous. He saw architecture as decorated structure: that is, determining the most appropriate structure for the requirements of plan and function and then clothing it with the most appropriate architecture.

following year Burnet commenced the construction of Atlantic Chambers (whose very name celebrated Glasgow's trade with America), and Charles Rennie Mackintosh his competition-winning Glasgow School of Art.

Like New York and Chicago, the commercial heart of Glasgow is based upon a grid-iron of city blocks, each comprising three or four plots. Commercial expansion required large areas of space on efficient floor plates, based upon the latest technology, so as to satisfy the needs of the *modern commercial user.* The advent of the mechanical lift, the commercial production of high-yield steel frames, and a review of the Fire Code provided the tools for a new architecture. In 1897 James Thomson completed the first of Glasgow's giant six-storey office blocks for the Pearl Assurance Company, in West George Street, the sophistication of his modern electric elevators

3 – The Rookery, Chicago, Burnham and Root, 1885-7

4 – Wainwright Building, Chicago, Adler and Sullivan

1 - Perrycroft, Malvern, C F A Voysey

2 - Machinery Hall, 1901 Glasgow International Exhibition

concealed behind a façade of Italianate and German Renaissance.

Thomson's building ran contrary to the new wave. Even Oscar Wilde, in 1882, had been enthused by modernity: *all machinery may be beautiful. Do not seek to decorate it. We cannot but think all good machinery is graceful: the line of strength and the line of beauty being one.* (1) Louis Sullivan applied a similar manifesto to buildings in his 1892 **Ornament in Architecture**: *Ornament is essentially a luxury, not a necessity ... It would be greatly to our aesthetic good if we should refrain entirely from the use of ornament for a period of years, in order that our thought might concentrate acutely on the production of building.* (2) The following year, approval of the unadorned form was endorsed by C F A Voysey when completing *Perrycroft* in the Malvern Hills: *Discarding the mass of useless ornaments would be healthy and desirable.* (3)

That Miller shared such values may be inferred from two of his rarely recorded sentiments: in 1901, that *the vital element of an architectural design is utility;* and his reiteration in 1924 that *the architecture of the exterior should be an expression of its character and purpose.* (4) In spite of such strikingly modern features as the consistently horizontal fenestration and the massive block shapes of Perrycroft's chimney stacks, it is nowhere demonstratively anti-traditional, and fits in perfectly with its natural surroundings.

Louis Sullivan regarded the design of the tall office building as a problem which contained and suggested its own solution, but which could not possibly be solved within established architectural rules, conventions and habit. Instead, he organised the building's mass, function and utility to suit a structural system which was carried through in structural clarity and use of materials. A contrast was therefore developed between an emphasised structure and the lightness and independence of any infill. Miller, who held that the vital element of all architectural design was utility, found Sullivan's

3

approach peculiarly appealing, as was to be exemplified in his later bank buildings.

Miller's early works, under the influence of George Graham and later Donald Matheson as chief engineers of the Caledonian Railway, respect utility. Matheson, having visited the USA and Canada in 1903 on behalf of the Caledonian Railway Company, also provided a North American influence. Work on these stations offered Miller the opportunity to develop his design approach with a particular understanding of the utility of structure, and the possibilities of high quality steel.

Between 1893-1914, the architecture of Scotland moved from exuberant decorative styles to simpler, more austere forms: from the Scots renaissance revivalism of Sir Robert Lorimer and Sir Robert Rowand Anderson to an architecture based upon structural clarity and utility of purpose. In *Das Englische Haus* Hermann Muthesius referred to Miller as one of *a small group of Scottish architects stirred by the wind of modernity* (5); and his best domestic work of the period reveals an evolution from Craighuchty Terrace, Aberfoyle to Forteviot Village in their economy of line, form and materials. As Pevsner noted of Voysey's Perrycroft: *all have strikingly modern features, consistently horizontal fenestration, massive block*

4

Rather than possessing architectural originality bursting with theory and ideas but lacking imaginative and daring clientele, Miller was a shrewd business-like professional who could command the design of any building and provide his clients with an efficient and stylish result. Consequently, his work was always in demand.

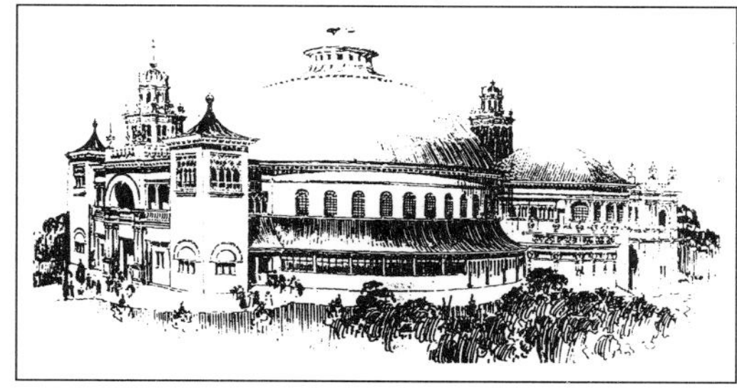

5

3 – Guaranty Building, Buffalo, Adler and Sullivan, 1894-6

4 – Detail, North British Locomotive Company, Glasgow

5 – Concert Hall, 1901 Glasgow International Exhibition

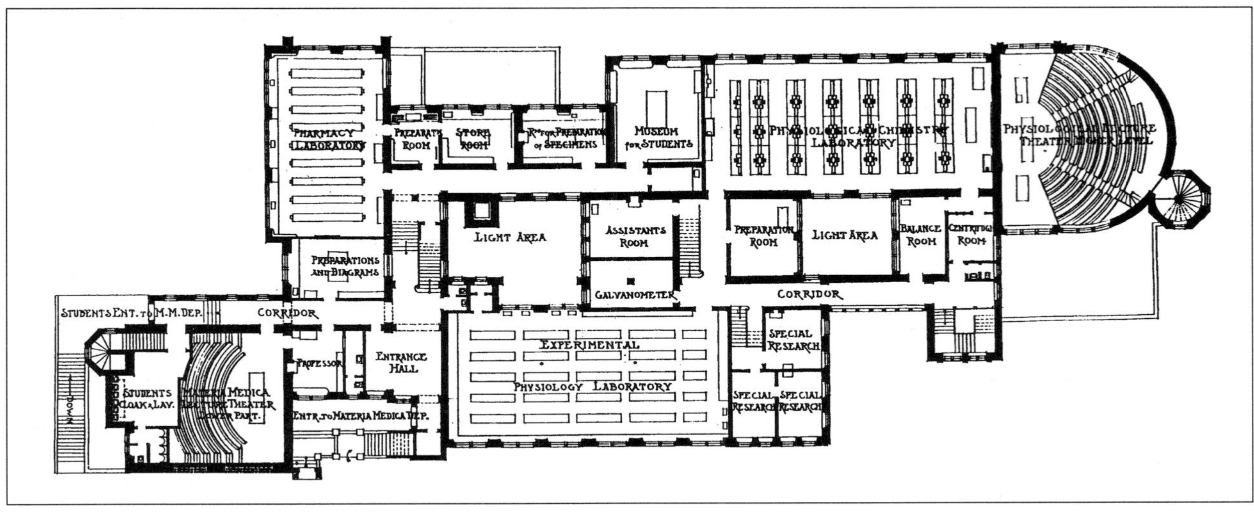

1

2

1 – **Plan, Materia Medica, Glasgow University**

2 – **Little Thakeham, Sussex, Lutyens, 1902**

shapes of chimney and gables but it is nowhere demonstratively anti-traditional. (6)

In Turnberry Hotel Miller took simple forms and subtlely articulated their surfaces by the restrained use of roofscapes, gables, dormers and bay windows (as did Lutyens in the Orchards, Munstead Woods and Papillion Hall, Leicestershire). Most strongly, the influence of Lutyens may be seen in his designs for the Barrhill mansion of Kildonan. Yet, in stark contrast to the picturesqueness of the Lutyens and Voysey houses, perhaps as a result of the climate, terrain or Scots Calvinism, they display a particular asceticism, devoid of unnecessary ornament, rational in approach and refined in detail.

At Forteviot, Miller refined his vocabulary, and stark simplicity, although not antithetical to the cottage tradition, is more redolent of a new European architecture than of rural Scotland. Masterly in proportion, a minimal palette is used to best effect.

Conflict between classicism and modernism became increasingly contentious from the turn of the century, which in 1935 Sir Giles Gilbert Scott expressed as the debate between the functionalism of the scientific mind, and the traditionalism of the romantic movement. Miller's attempt, as always combining technical advancement with stylistic trends, to resolve the

3

More important to Miller than stylistic detail and compositional ideas was consistent approach to design: ***Mr Miller believes that in their elements, architecture and engineering are the same, what difference there is lying in the former adding what may be called the graphic or pictorial element to the latter, harmonising all parts and appealing to the senses more directly.*** **(7)**

4

two reached its apogee in the Commercial Bank in Bothwell Street: perhaps his finest commercial building.

His practice then embarked on a series of more utilitarian public buildings, in a functionalist aesthetic responding to the white horizontality of post-Weissenhof Europe. It can be seen in the RSNI Larbert Colony, 1934, Canniesburn Hospital, 1935, and the Ear Nose and Throat Hospital, Greenock, 1937. Canniesburn's proportions are horizontal, counterpointed by the entrance tower and flanking towers.

What is certain in any overview of his work is a consistent strand of development, utility and purpose. His buildings are restrained in architectural expression whilst embracing contemporary technology. All exhibit the primacy of structural clarity over any decorative tradition. Where decoration is allowed to dominate, the work is generally less successful, when compared to the work of his contemporaries more scholarly in the architecture of the Scots Renaissance revival.

Each design is a complex and sometimes eclectic enterprise, trying to combine the needs of the client with expanding a series of architectural ideas. There is a symbiosis between innovation and tradition. Even if Miller rarely innovated

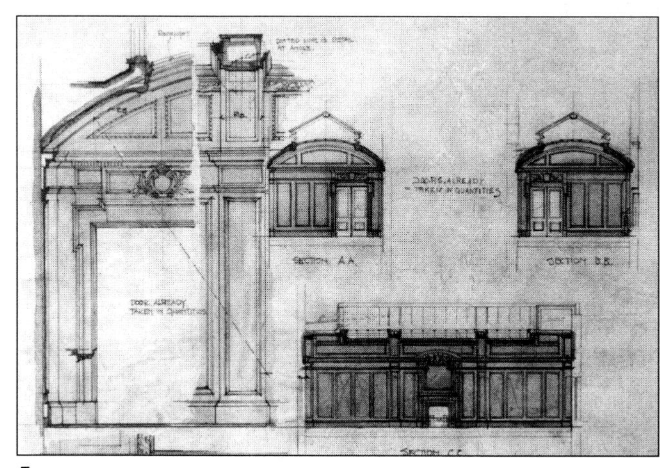

5

3 – Ranfurly Hotel, Bridge of Weir. Miller was commissioned to carry out alterations to the hotel

4 – House at Weissenhofsiedlung, Stuttgart, Hans Scharoun, 1927

5 – Detail of panelling in Council Dining Room, Institution of Civil Engineers, London

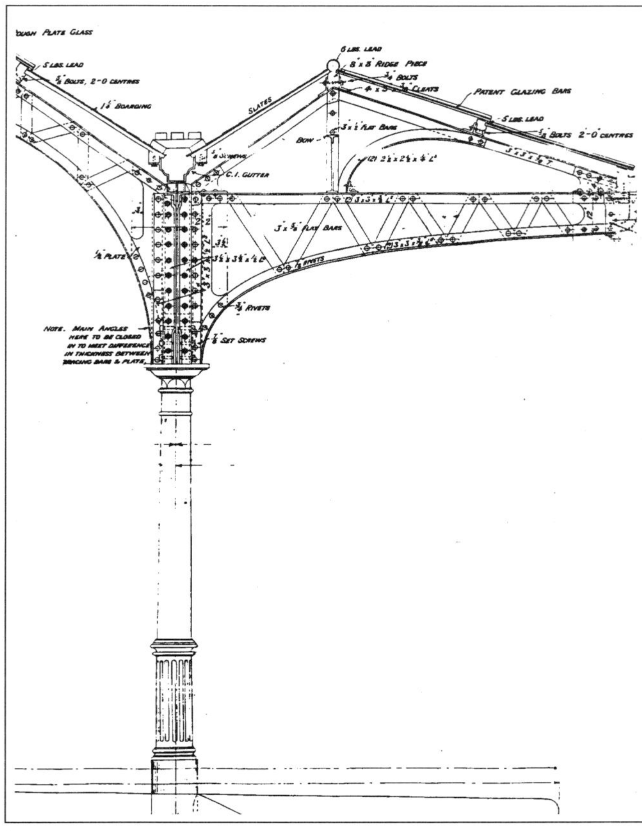

1

2

1 – Detail, roof support, Wemyss Bay Railway Station

2 – Bentinck Drive, Troon

conceptually, he synthesised ideas shared with his contemporaries. He then adapted them to a specific programme, and overlaid them with quotations from both historical and contemporary sources.

Otherwise, little is known about Miller's opinions. A modest man, he was known to prefer to stand in the background, out of the limelight, when attending the opening ceremonies of buildings which he had designed. (8) *Very reserved by nature, he did not enter much into public life, and was well content to let others talk architecture while he was doing the job. Quick-tempered, he could also be very sympathetic and understanding when the occasion demanded. He was a hard task-master, although few of the men who passed through his hands would deny that they benefited to a remarkable degree.* (9) Amongst those who passed through those capable hands were James Bell, James Carrick (both father and son), Alexander Dunlop, James Walker, and George Boswell. Richard Gunn, who became chief assistant in the office in 1918 and remained there until his death in 1933, was valued by Miller as *a brilliant and rapid craftsman, scholarly and refined* in design. (10)

Miller married Emilina Crichton and had three children – George (later to join the practice), Mabel (sponsor of this book) and Muriel. He lived first in 3 Hillhead Gardens (19 Hillhead Street), a terraced house in Glasgow's West End, before moving in 1911 to Randolphfield, an 18th-century laird's house on the outskirts of Stirling. He travelled daily to his office at 15 Blythswood Square, either by rail (from Stirling Station, which he rebuilt 1912-15 for the Caledonian Company, replacing an earlier one by Andrew Heiton) or in some style by car, either a Hispano Suiza or Delage driven by his chauffeur Mustard. Such was the status of the Hispano Suiza that when the Millers gifted the car to the local fire brigade to assist the war effort, it was transformed into a fire engine. Pruning the roses in Randolphfield's extensive grounds or playing the violin were Miller's preferred relaxations, and when his schedule permitted, he played with his children at

2

3

croquet, took them fishing, built them a tennis court in the garden and taught them to play golf both at the local course and at Gleneagles.

George's death from ill health in 1940 impelled Miller toward retiral since he saw no reason to continue working without an heir to take over the practice. In 1943 he was awarded the unique honour of an Honorary Fellowship of the Royal Incorporation of Architects in Scotland (when already a Fellow) for his outstanding contribution to 20th-century Scottish architecture. He died four years later, on 28 November 1947, aged 87, at Randolphfield. His ashes were laid, appropriately, in the Kirk of the Holy Rude, which he had taken such pains to restore.

The practice was taken over by John Wellwood Manson as Miller & Manson. Educated at the Glasgow School of Art and the Royal College of Technology, Manson had served his apprenticeship with George Boswell, one of Miller's former assistants. A watercolour painter in his spare time, Manson continued the practice until an early death in 1953 aged 50. Frank Burnet Bell & Partners, successor practice to Burnet & Boston, took over the outstanding work. In 1984 James Rennie, the senior partner, donated Miller's drawings to the RIAS Drawings Collection.

2 - Rose garden, Randolphfield, Stirling

3 - Dining Room, 19 Hillhead Street, Glasgow

James Miller 1888 – 1900

1

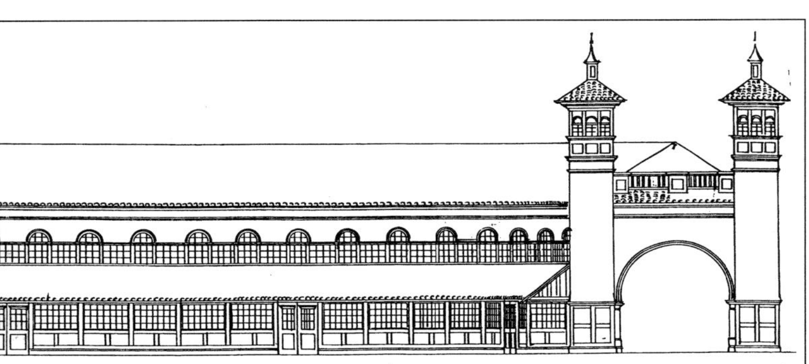

2

1 – Interior, Stirling Railway Station

2 – Princes Pier Railway Station and Steamer Terminal, Greenock

In 1888 James Miller joined the drawing office of the Caledonian Railway Company at a time when the railway companies had become powerful empires. Valuable city centre land was devoured, and new rail networks extended the boundaries of Glasgow, stretching the suburbs deeper into the countryside and spawning commuter towns and villages far from the pollution and noise of the city. The Caledonian's lines down the west coast encouraged leisure travel, and a string of seaside resorts developed to exploit seasonal tourism, feeding upon the prosperity of the metropolis. For the character of many of the stations on these lines, often significant buildings in their communities, Miller was responsible.

The earliest was **Bridge Street Station**, Glasgow, 1889-90, undertaken with the company's engineer, George Graham: a rigorous 18-bay, grey stone façade on the ground floor flanked by arched entrances to the high-level platforms behind. It is now barely recognisable as a railway station, closed following the completion of the extension to **Central Station** in 1905.

Miller favoured a simple, English domestic for rural stations like **Fort Matilda** (1889), **Troon** (1892) and **West Kilbride** (1900): brick harl or tile-hung walls, pitched roofs, and gables etched with bold black and white half-timbering.

Tourists who wished to venture *doon the water*, across to Helensburgh, Rothesay or Dunoon, required rail/steamer terminal buildings adequate to cope with the sheer volume of holidaymakers at the height of the summer season. Those were much grander architectural affairs. **Gourock Pier Railway Station**, 1889 (since partially demolished), was the most advanced of its time (1): 20 half-timbered gables and a sturdy clock tower overlooking the Clyde acted as a superb beacon for the steamers drawing up parallel to the trains at the quayside.

Miller's **Princes Pier** in Greenock, 1893, for the rival **Glasgow and South Western Railway Company** (demolished 1967), was enlivened by six square Italianate towers. The two larger

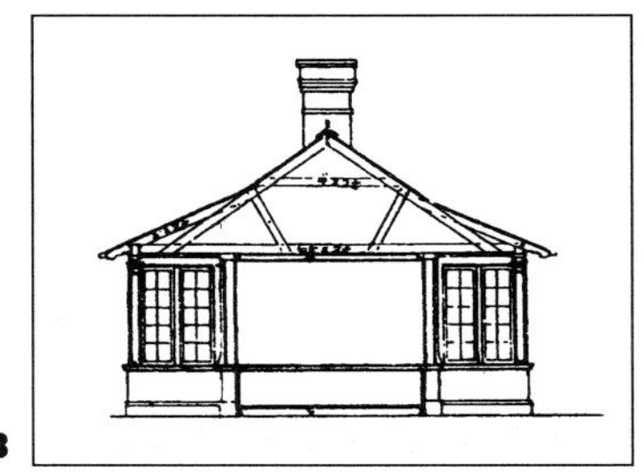

3

4

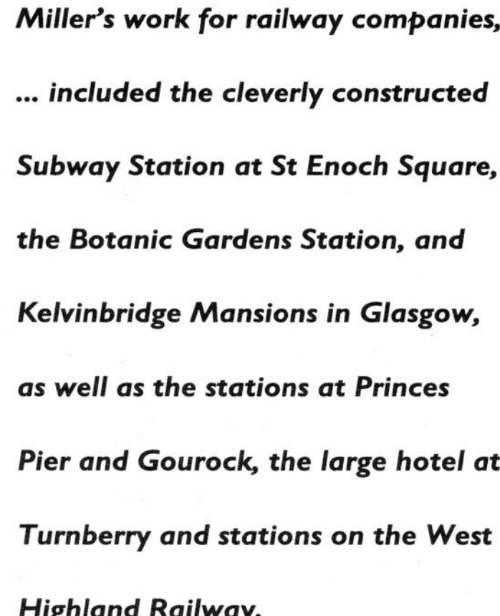

Miller's work for railway companies, ... included the cleverly constructed Subway Station at St Enoch Square, the Botanic Gardens Station, and Kelvinbridge Mansions in Glasgow, as well as the stations at Princes Pier and Gourock, the large hotel at Turnberry and stations on the West Highland Railway.

Glasgow Herald, 1st December 1947

5

towers containing circular stairs flanked the central booking office, whose balcony overlooked the water. Wings stretched out on either side, sweeping round and down to enfold the boats at the pierside, terminating in large arched doorways, each flanked by two smaller decorative towers with little pyramid roofs. Curving walls for the circulation of passengers were to reappear in later stations, such as **Wemyss Bay**, **Stirling** and the enlarged concourse at **Central Station**.

The Caledonian Company absorbed the Glasgow Central Railway Company soon after its formation in 1888, and planned a low-level line through the city. The engineer responsible for the complicated tunnelling required through the streets of the city was Donald Matheson, with whom Miller designed

3 – West Highland Railway Station attributed to Miller

4 – Botanic Gardens low-level Station, Glasgow

5 – West Kilbride Railway Station

1

1 – 1901 Glasgow International Exhibition

two stations: **Kelvinbridge** and the **Botanic Gardens**, both of 1896. The former (demolished after a fire in 1968) was built on two levels (2): at the upper level, overlooking Caledonian Crescent, a curious brick pavilion welcomed passengers through twin-arched doorways, in a gable split by a prominent central chimney. The buildings were signalled by a jaunty, diminutive circulate tower capped with an ogee roof and finial (a feature to reappear in **St Enoch's**, 1896, and in nearby **Caledonian Mansions**, 1897).

Tracking the tunnel west along Great Western Road we emerge at the **Botanic Gardens Station** – much more of an architectural extravaganza. Red brick and half-timbered gables flanking the main pavilion were familiar elements, but the two pagoda-like clock towers, each with a decorative projecting balcony girdling a bulbous gilded dome, were most extraordinary. Miller was

2

3

to enjoy dabbling in oriental architecture again in the **Glasgow International Exhibition**, 1901. (3)

Yet, architectural convention conflicted with subterranean demands from the engineers: the building service core, with its two sets of stairs down to the low-level platforms, was set at an oblique angle to the main shell of the building, creating awkward spaces within the booking hall. Architect and engineer learned later to work in greater harmony. The low-level line remained unpopular: dirty and smoky due to poor ventilation, it could not compete with the subway, trams and motorcars and it closed to passengers in 1939. The station's conversion to a tearoom prolonged its life until demolished after a fire in 1970.

It was not only Miller's approach to railway architecture that was influenced by his time with the Caledonian Railway; he also applied railway style to his early domestic work. The English Arts & Crafts movement was perfect for houses in the idyllic, newly-formed Glasgow suburbs. It was a language with which he was at ease, as can be seen in **Dunloskin, Dumbreck**, Glasgow, 1890, a superb example of Miller's English Arts & Crafts style: prominent chimneys and gables, half-timbering and tile-hung walls. It was illustrated in *The Architect* 7 February 1902 with mature ivy smothering one of the bay windows, highlighting

4

2 – Canadian Pavilion, 1901 Glasgow International Exhibition

3 – Dunloskin, Dumbreck, Glasgow

4 – Craighuchty Terrace, Aberfoyle

1

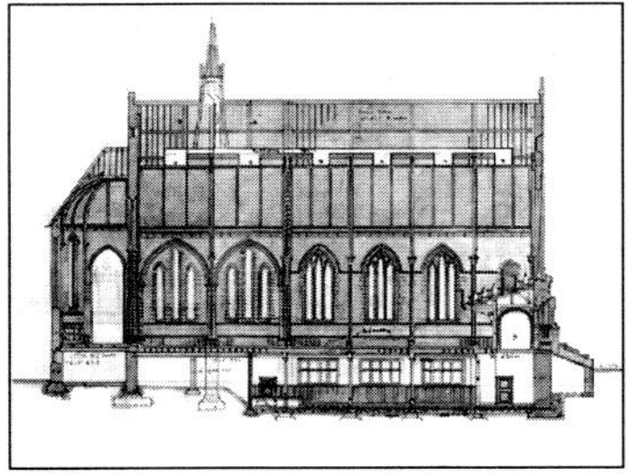

2

1 – South elevation, St Enoch Subway Station, St Enoch Square, Glasgow

2 – Belmont Parish Church, Great George Street, Glasgow

its picturesque qualities. **Craighuchty Terrace**, Aberfoyle, *c.*1890, is a striking row of six houses in the same vein: red sandstone on the ground, tile-hung above. Subtle changes in the rhythm of the façade are achieved by the half-timbered gables – larger ones projecting over bay windows, the smaller flush with the tile-hung wall but piercing the eaves. Each house has a personal identity, although, collectively, the composition reads like a single house or hotel.

Winning the competition for the design of **Belmont Parish Church**, 121 Great George Street, Hillhead, Glasgow, in 1893, enabled Miller to break away from the Caledonian Railway Company to form his own practice. A red sandstone church in Early English Gothic with delicate Scottish tracery, its aisle-less cruciform plan had similarities to Burnet's Barony Church. (4) Belmont now forms part of Laurelbank School.

Miller also continued to design for the Caledonian Railway Company, and developed a close working relationship with Donald Matheson, who had succeeded George Graham as the company's chief engineer. Miller undertook many major contracts for the company directors and received several prestigious commissions from their friends. They did not seem to mind him designing for their rivals, as he did in his next commission, **St Enoch Subway Station**, 1896, for the Glasgow and District Subway Company. Their new circular underground railway was in direct competition with the Caledonian's expensive low-level line: it was advertised as the *only underground cable railway in the world – no smoke, no steam, perfect ventilation*. (5) Although initially successful, it too suffered stiff competition from the trams until its electrification in 1939.

Miller's design for the station at St Enoch Square is a plucky little red sandstone, Scots Renaissance château, crammed with detail. The ground floor housed ticket booth, book stall and stairs which led to platforms below. The first floor accommodated offices and it is at this level that the façade comes alive: circular, copper ogee-capped turrets wrestle with balconies and oriel windows projected on larger brackets.

3

St Mary's Episcopal Church, Aberfoyle, c.1893, has harled walls, red sandstone dressings, half-timbering, bellcote and tiny, pitched roof with finial.

4

A similar combination of Jacobean and Scottish informs **Caledonian Mansions**, 445-459 Great Western Road, Glasgow, 1897, for the Caledonian Railway Company. Conveniently adjacent to Kelvinbridge Station, it was originally proposed as an annexe to the Caledonian Hotel (prior to the extension of Central Station several years later) but now accommodates flats and ground-floor shops. The elevation to Great Western Road is broadly symmetrical. The ogee-capped tourelles with finials are inflated versions of those at St Enoch's and the Kelvinbridge Station that it overlooked. Its prominent chimneys, oriel windows, gables and dormer windows, all varying in size, form a vivid insertion amidst the more regular west-end tenements. The rear is even more playful. Large stone brackets support a projecting access balcony running across much of the elevation; windows have corbelled brackets with semi-circular panels above, and arched doorways to the flats echo the cavernous mouth of the railway tunnel below. The building celebrates the River Kelvin with more ogee roofs, oriel windows, cantilevered balconies, prominent chimneys and a decoratively carved gable.

Miller's first essay at design on a grand scale can

5

3 – St Mary's Episcopal Church, Aberfoyle

4 – Front elevation, Caledonian Mansions, Great Western Road, Glasgow

5 – Rear elevation, Caledonian Mansions

1

2

1 – Belfast City Hall, competition entry

2 – Clydebank Municipal Buildings, Dumbarton Road, Glasgow

be seen in his unsuccessful competition entry for **Belfast City Hall**, an enormous baroque design clearly influenced by Young's Glasgow City Chambers (particularly the central and corner

3

towers). It was one of the three designs placed by the competition assessor, Alfred Waterhouse, but the winning design was that by Brumwell Thomas, who had used St Paul's Cathedral and Greenwich Hospital as sources for his grand *central* dome. (6)

Clydebank Municipal Buildings, Dumbarton Road, Clydebank, 1893-1902, provided Miller with a new challenge: a civic monument for a booming burgh, as Clydebank enjoyed the peak of Clyde shipbuilding. Initial plans were rejected and a limited number of architects were invited to submit designs for new offices and chambers in a competition judged by William Leiper. Miller won, and almost immediately had to revise the scheme due to further population expansion. Construction began in 1900 and included a town hall and municipal offices, police department, public baths, fire station and dwellings, library and burgh court room. Baroque in style, it is dominated by a corner tower rising up from a rather plain stone base to an open cupola (reminiscent of those at William Young's Glasgow City Chambers, 1883-8, and the 1901 Exhibition) which houses a carillon of bells. At one time it was adorned by the figure of *Mercury* (taken from the entrance of the 1901 Glasgow International Exhibition) representing the

4

3 – Coupar Grange in Perthshire, c.1900, a simple and disciplined exterior in English vernacular Jacobean

4 – Interior, Coupar Grange

1

2

3

1 - Interior, Coupar Grange, Perthshire

2 - Drawing room, Miller's house at 19 Hillhead Street, Glasgow, c.1900. The wallpaper is tastefully stencilled above the dado line, more Glasgow Style than the French and Jacobean he designed for his clients

3 - Lintwhite School, Lintwhite Crescent, Bridge of Weir

triumph of engineering, an appropriate gesture for the area. Removed after storm damage in 1968, the statue now stands in the main entrance hall. The entrance from Hall Street combines baroque with art nouveau: two squat towers, each with a heavy cornice, project from the main façade, flanking a large arched window above the door. This Miller motif is crowned by a segmental pediment, broken by an obelisk (a Norman Shaw motif used by J J Burnet at the Athenaeum Theatre).

The house in **Bentinck Drive**, Troon, c.1900, designed for the whisky magnate, Sir Alexander Walker of Johnnie Walker, is Arts & Crafts, with harled walls, deep overhanging eaves, bargeboards, and a tile-hung gable at the front. The battered wall at the main entrance betrays a more obvious art nouveau influence. Sir Alexander Walker, a key figure in the local community, was one of the committee members who commissioned Miller's design of the **Municipal Buildings** at South Beach, Troon, 1930.

Art nouveau was rarely displayed by Miller's work, perhaps because of its inappropriateness to his main commissions. However, it is present in features such as the battered chimneys and wide gently curving bay windows of his competition-winning design for **Lintwhite School**, Lintwhite Crescent, Bridge of Weir, 1900. It accommodated six classrooms for between 20 and 50 pupils, with movable glass partitions for flexibility. (7) Designed on an H-plan, with a central main hall with an open timber roof, this charming red sandstone building has been converted to flats and houses.

In 1898 James Miller won the competition for the **1901 Glasgow International Exhibition**, just

4

5

6

The Glasgow International Exhibition is situated in Kelvingrove Park and adjoining grounds – almost one hundred acres being enclosed.

1901 Glasgow International Exhibition brochure

five years after setting up practice. Fourteen competition entries were submitted, including one by Charles Rennie Mackintosh, but Miller's romantic, rather Americanised, 16th-century Spanish Renaissance had popular appeal. Although such a backward-looking language for an exhibition which represented the latest in world technology may seem strange today, it offered Glaswegians a form of escapism, particularly with its use of all-pervading white, inspired by the 1893 *White City* exhibition in Chicago.

Generally, the pavilions were made of prefabricated plaster panels, on a base of sacking, were nailed to timber frames and stuccoed over. It was light and simple to work with, perfect for a temporary exhibition but unsuitable for enduring the Glasgow weather for long.

The six very unusual buildings making up the Russian Village were by Shekhtel, who also supervised the work of the 180 Russian peasants who slowly built it. The greens, reds, blues and salmon, with gilding and silvering, would have been a lovely contrast to the white of Miller's main exhibition buildings. (8)

7

4 – House for Alexander Walker, Bentinck Drive, Troon

5 – Russian Village, 1901 Glasgow International Exhibition

6 – Concert Hall, 1901 Glasgow International Exhibition

7 – Industrial Hall, Museum and Art Galleries, 1901 Glasgow International Exhibition

James Miller 1901 – 1914

1

GLASGOW INTERNATIONAL EXHIBITION.

PATRON, HIS MAJESTY THE KING.

ART.
SCIENCE.
INDUSTRY.
COMMERCE.

2

1 – Industrial Hall, 1901 Glasgow International Exhibition

2 – Brochure from 1901 Glasgow International Exhibition

Nothing remains of the exhibition save tiny cottages perched on the river bank near Glasgow University, a replica of houses from **Port Sunlight** in Cheshire. This cheerful paradigm of wholesome, idealised life in the modern English garden suburb, with its black and white, half-timbered, red-brick and tile-hung walls, may have been unusual for Glasgow, but the language was familiar to Miller. It was a gift to the city of Glasgow from Lord Leverhume, and remained a reminder of the grand affair once the exhibition was dismantled, and Spanish palaces replaced by leafy avenues (*see p.C4*).

The publicity generated by the 1901 exhibition led to a series of commissions, of which **Nos 8-10 Lowther Terrace**, Great Western Road, Glasgow was the first. This row of three houses begun in 1900 was never completed as originally planned. Unlike nearby **Lancaster Crescent**,

4

3

Its object is to present a full illustration of the British Empire, its dependencies, dominions, and colonies, and the progress in industry, science, and art of all nationalities during the nineteenth century

1901 Glasgow International Exhibition brochure

Opening of the Glasgow International Exhibition 1901.

THE LORD PROVOST AND CORPORATION
OF THE CITY OF GLASGOW
request the honour of the Company of

Mr James Miller

AT LUNCHEON, IN THE CITY CHAMBERS, ON THURSDAY, THE SECOND MAY,
AT TWO O'CLOCK, AFTER THE OPENING OF THE EXHIBITION, TO MEET
Her Royal Highness the Princess Louise, Duchess of Fife
and His Grace the Duke of Fife.

City Chambers,
Glasgow, April, 1901.

Official or Morning Dress.

An early reply is requested to
The City Chamberlain.

5

c.1898, where Miller designed **No 2**, and three other architects – Henry Higgins, J L Conran, J C McKellar – created a series of nine similar units, Lowther Terrace comprised individual Jacobean Renaissance essays bonded by scale to create a single impressive composition.

No 10 Lowther Terrace, the first to be built, was extended to the west in 1904 and 1909 to add a conservatory and a billiard room with a barrel-vaulted ceiling. A large, shaped gable dominates the asymmetrical four-storey façade. At first-floor level a projecting balcony with plain metal balustrades butts against the two-storey bay window, providing shelter for the main entrance below. The centre house, No 9, was designed by

3 – Captured Boer gun at the Exhibition

4 – Main Entrance, Industrial Hall, 1901 Glasgow International Exhibition

5 – Invitation to the opening

1

2

3

1 - 8-10 Lowther Terrace, Kelvinside, Glasgow

2 - Elevation of 8 Lowther Terrace

3 - Adam Bedroom, 10 Lowther Terrace

Sydney Mitchell in 1904-6, at the same time as Miller designed **No 8** – whose centrally-positioned bay window rises a full three storeys, butted on either side by projecting balconies supported by Doric columns. All houses were joined in a conversion by Noad & Wallace to a Church of Scotland old people's home in 1948.

Between 1901 and 1908 the Caledonian Company, whose Central Station badly needed to expand to cope with the sheer volume of travellers, appointed Miller, with his extensive railway experience, as the architect alongside the chief engineer Donald Matheson in the design of major extensions.

Miller enjoyed a good working relationship with Matheson, who was the same age and likewise a pupil at Perth Academy, and his penchant for engineering would have been strengthened by it. In 1903 Matheson had been dispatched to the United States and Canada to observe the latest techniques in railway building. He was impressed by the use of curved walls, which enabled people to *travel along the line of least resistance* and thereby circulate more freely (1), whence developed the new, rounded, timber panelled kiosks dotted around the spacious concourse, and the *Torpedo*

4

Miller was much influenced by D A Matheson, chief engineer of the Caledonian Railway Company, first as mentor, then as client – a relationship that reached its peak in their collaboration on Central Station, from which Miller gained a particular understanding of utility and of the potential of the high quality steel then becoming available. From then on, Miller moved gradually away from the revivalism of the Robert Rowand Anderson school to a simpler architecture based upon structural clarity. No frills: each element carrying an appropriate weight in the composition.

5

6

building, which accommodated the indicator boards and waiting room (now converted into the Caledonian Centre with bar, restaurant and shops). Unlike the station at Botanic Gardens, the building form was at last allied to function, a bond between architecture and engineering which culminated at Wemyss Bay Station in 1904.

Between 1900 and 1905 Miller extended Rowand Anderson's Central Station Hotel in Hope Street, enveloping Matheson's new *French* semi-elliptical girders over the new platforms to the west. (2) The extension along Hope Street is barely distinguishable from the 1883 façade, as Miller repeated Anderson's Florentine and Jacobean details throughout much of the elevation. He also designed a lounge curving out over the concourse above the booking hall, with a dome *supported* by

4 – Central Station Hotel extension, Hope Street, Glasgow

5 – Concourse, Central Station during the 1920s

6 – Elevation of Hope Street extension of Central Station Hotel

1

Ionic columns and glazed by Oscar Paterson (who had created the staircase window at 10 Lowther Terrace, 1900). (3) Miller also designed a screen of early Italian windows for the train hall overlooking Hope Street and a rich early Renaissance façade for the *Highlandman's Umbrella* over Argyle Street with its huge windows articulated by colourful iron pilasters.

2

Caledonian Chambers, Union Street, Glasgow, 1901-3, was designed as the Caledonian Railway Company's offices, and dominates Union Street, ground0floor shops flanking an entrance to the station. The first floor provided additional station accommodation: a waiting room, a smoking room and a roof-lit dining room overlooking the concourse. Bay windows at the first and second storeys support a balcony running the length of the main façade, breaking only at the pediment of the aedicule over the central doorway. Above, an Ionic colonnade marches across eleven bays of coupled windows. The flanking towers are more deeply modelled, with the coupled columns of the two-storey armorial aedicules supported by two Michelangesque figures by Albert Hodge, a sculptor who worked with Miller on several occasions. The upper windows in the towers are recessed, and framed by an arch (a technique used for highlighting the end bays of the North British Locomotive Company Offices, 1909).

1 – Highlandman's Umbrella, Argyle Street, Glasgow

2 – Caledonian Chambers, Union Street, Glasgow

Wemyss Bay Railway Station, 1904, Miller's most successful railway building, exercises Matheson's theories about passenger circulation

3

most beautifully. The focal point of the concourse is the circular booking office, where the roof fans out from the building like a great umbrella (see *pp.C2, C4*). From this point a timber walkway curves gently down to the steamer pier, ending in a pair of stumpy towers which echo the Italianate clocktower on the main façade (a symbolic gesture developed from earlier terminal buildings at Princes Pier and Gourock). The extensive use of

4

glazing enables holidaymakers returning from Rothesay or Millport to savour the last drop of precious blue sky, and contemplate the graceful forms of the elliptical steel roof trusses before boarding the train back to Glasgow. Bold half-timbering above a red sandstone base creates a distinct vertical emphasis to the façade. Each timber strip transforms into a bracket to support the cornice, a square clock above. A pyramid roof with large overhanging eaves and weather vane, completes the ensemble. Although the exterior is typical of Miller's other railway work along the Clyde coast, the materials demonstrate a clear hierarchy: red sandstone for doors and windows and as a solid base for gently curving white-harled walls, topped by half-timbered gables.

The replacement of Robert Adam's **Glasgow Royal Infirmary**, 106 Castle Street, between 1901 and 1907, proved to be controversial and a target of considerable public criticism – due partly

The Executive Committee was adamant: ***It is distinctively Scottish, the national style of the 15th and 16th centuries of which we have examples in Heriot's Hospital, Holyrood Palace and Falkland Palace. It is therefore, not only appropriate to the historical associations of the site upon which stood the castellated Bishop's Palace, but permitting as it does a limited use of Gothic forms, it is more in harmony with the Cathedral itself than any classic or modern style.*** **(4)**

5

3 – Early proposal for Glasgow Royal Infirmary

4 – Interior, Wemyss Bay Railway Station

5 – Elevation, Wemyss Bay Railway Station

to the sensitivity of the site adjacent to Glasgow Cathedral, and partly to the mishandling of the architectural competition.

The Committee required that the hospital should be rebuilt with minimum inconvenience to the existing patients. The ten competitors were even given a sketch plan on which they were expected to base their designs. Sir Rowand Anderson, the eminent technical advisor appointed to guide the Committee in their decision, recommended H E Clifford as the winner of the competition. The Committee disagreed, however, undermining his professional opinion by offering the commission instead to Miller, who, unlike the other entrants, had followed their sketch plans very closely. The three powerful perspective drawings submitted with his design would undoubtedly have helped sway the Committee in his favour. (5)

It was an unpopular outcome. The sheer bulk of the new Infirmary was thought to overshadow the Cathedral, and Miller's baronial style inappropriate for a modern hospital.

1 - Perspective, Glasgow Royal Infirmary, Castle Street

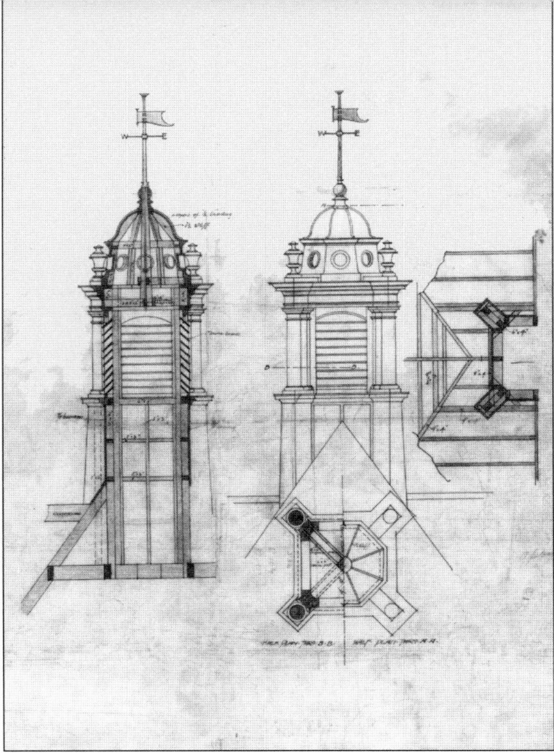

3

2

The vent tower was first used on the Royal Infirmary, 1901-7, the Natural Philosophy Building at Glasgow University, 1903-7 and on Turnberry Hotel, 1904-7. The cupola type ventilation tower is constructed completely in timber with a leaded roof. The details, construction and function have been replicated on all the above buildings almost as standard detail or practice signature.

As the design developed, many baronial elements were stripped: turrets were replaced by baroque cupolas and crenellations superseded by balustrades. (6) A few Scottish elements – such as the bartizaned square towers in the centre and the huge circular towers (which functioned as lavatories) – were retained. The overall effect was akin to Burnet's Scots Renaissance designs of the 1890s. Only the Queen's Diamond Jubilee Block, overlooking Cathedral Square, is entirely beaux arts in profile, an inflated version of the original hospital by Adam, with rustication, giant columns, mansard roof and central dome.

The Infirmary illustrates Miller's approach to design as decorated structure. Structure and functional resolution were of primary consideration, façade a secondary matter. Despite the adverse publicity, the Infirmary proved to be highly profitable for Miller: not only did later extensions provide work for his practice on and off until his retirement, but it also gave him valuable experience for his other hospitals. Features like the roof promenade and open balconies for convalescing patients reappeared in more stylish forms in his hospital work during the 1920s and '30s.

In 1903 Miller won the closely contested competition for the **Materia Medica and Physiology Buildings** at Glasgow University with a Scots Renaissance design, using blue Westmorland slates and white Giffnock stone. Its details were akin to those of the original Old College in the High Street. (7)

4

2 – Ventilator, Turnberry Hotel

3 – Ventilator detail, Natural Philosophy Building, Glasgow University

4 – Perspective, Materia Medica Buildings, Glasgow University

1

2

3

1 - Entrance, Natural Philosophy Building, Glasgow University

2 - St Andrew's East Church, Alexandra Parade, Dennistoun, Glasgow

3 - Elevation, St Andrew's East Church

For the two-storey **Natural Philosophy Building**, Glasgow University, 1903-6, Miller selected English Jacobean focussed on the main entrance: strapwork over the Doric doorpiece and first-floor window, and a cupola crowning the gabled roof. At the flanking bays, fluted, Ionic pilasters articulate the windows and the whole is crowned by a balustraded parapet. Glasgow University Court preferred Miller's design for its *simplicity and suitability beside the existing buildings.* (8) That view, also expressed by some of his other clients, highlighted Miller's ability to grasp the fundamentals of each brief.

St Andrew's East Church, 681-685 Alexandra Parade, Dennistoun, Glasgow, 1903-4, was erected after the church hall at the east was built in 1899 by James Salmon Jnr. With its formidable buttressed towers and battlements, this stalwart building is one of Miller's best and most original churches. (9) There is, as in his 1902 MacGregor Memorial Church, Govan, a smattering of art nouveau, seen in the character of the square bellcote and the battered walls of the towers above the spring of the single-arch spanning between. This arch casts a deep shadow over the recessed central window above the two doorways. Nowhere in Miller's other work is the combination of tower, arch and entrance quite as bold. For the bellcote he took the clock tower from the station at Wemyss Bay, petrified its vertical timber ribs and brackets and introduced an expressive curve into the profile of the roof.

Miller's majestic **Peebles Hydro**, 1904-5, replaced a hotel destroyed in a fire. It has a style

4

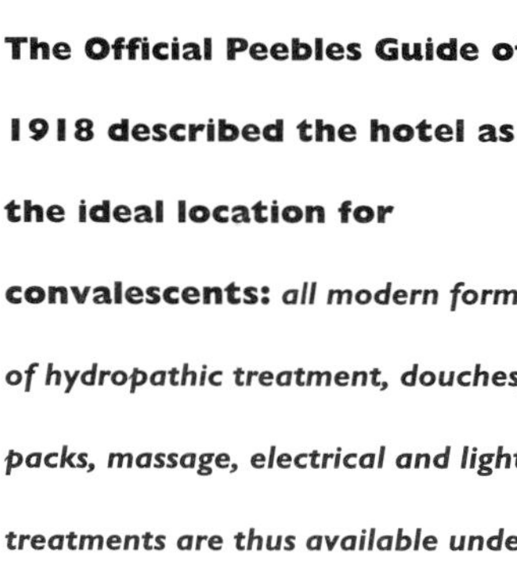
The Official Peebles Guide of 1918 described the hotel as the ideal location for convalescents: *all modern forms of hydropathic treatment, douches, packs, massage, electrical and light treatments are thus available under one roof.*

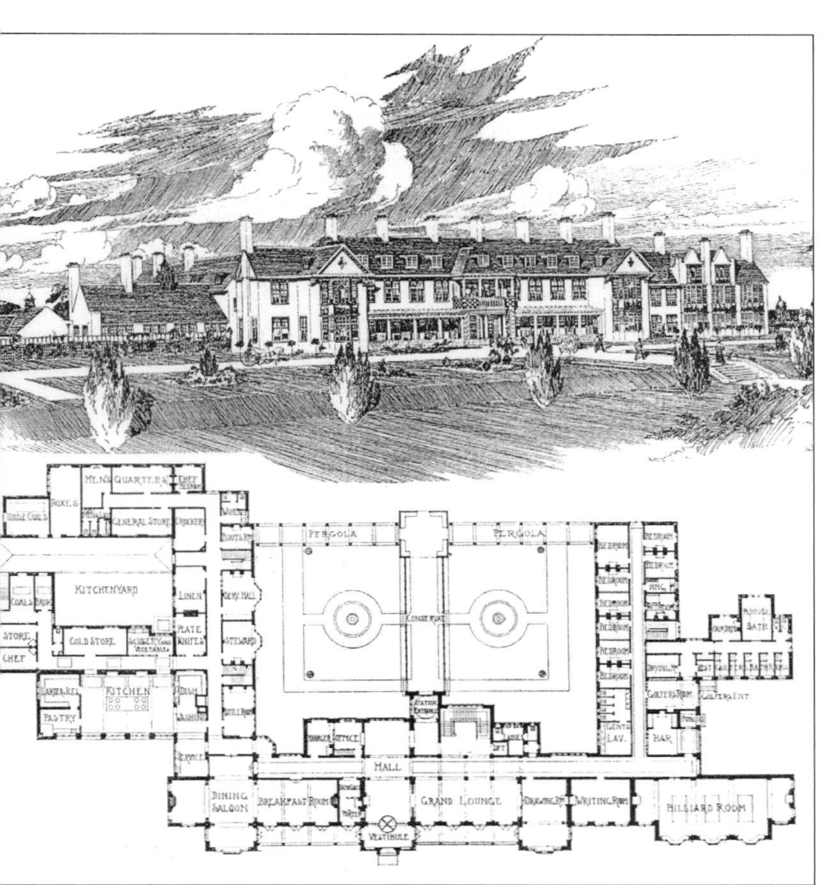

5

and grandeur which would make it equally at home in the Rocky Mountains of Canada, its formality enhanced by its setting on a plateau, with grassy terraces and a grand set of stairs leading the visitor up to the *porte cochère* (*see p.C4*). Queen Anne details lighten a three-storey façade, punctuated by projecting wings and dominated by a steep, hipped, red tile roof with two tiers of attic windows.

The exuberant **Turnberry Hotel**, built 1904-5 for the Glasgow and South Western Railway Company, who extended their railway line along the coast, was planned as a superior seaside holiday destination for Glaswegians, with a world-class links golf course (*see p.C1*).

It is not unlike a large English country house of the turn of the century. Like Peebles, its formality is enhanced by a hillside setting overlooking the golf course to Ailsa Craig. Although an offbeat

6

4 - Peebles Hydro

5 - Perspective and plan, Turnberry Hotel, Ayrshire

6 - Entrance, Turnberry Hotel

1

2

symmetry co-exists on the sea elevation with a centrally located entrance, the principal entrance is from the railway, bedroom wings on each side, creating a sheltered courtyard. One of Miller's finest works, the hotel embodies his theories of simplicity and utility of design. The façades are very simple, yet the composition as a whole is finely articulated.

Olympic House, a large 1903 speculative office development on the corner of Queen Street and George Square in Glasgow, was Miller's next large urban design. Like Caledonian Chambers, it has shops on the ground floor, but is simpler in style, moving toward a plainer, more American, commercial architecture. A corner tower flanks each elevation; the colonnades at the upper three storeys give a strong vertical emphasis, the entablature raising the design a further storey to a parapet adorned by a swag. The central portion of each façade at the fifth and sixth storeys is recessed, highlighting the Doric colonnades and the punchy rhythm of the attic above. A curious arcade spans the towers of the George Square elevation, framing a section of Glasgow skyline, like those linking the wards at Glasgow Royal Infirmary.

1 - Entrance, Turnberry Hotel, Ayrshire

2 - Offices, George Square/ Queen Street, Glasgow

2

1

1 - Balcony detail, Caledonian Mansions, 445-459 Great Western Road, Glasgow

2 - Turnberry Hotel set against a backdrop of hills

3 - Entrance, Turnberry Hotel

4 - Kildonan standing proud in its setting

3

4

1

2

3

4

1 - Oeil-de-boeuf window framed by swags, Woodhouse Warehouse (Prudential Assurance Building), 28-36 Renfield Street, Glasgow

2 - Ardlonish, Sutherland Avenue, Pollokshields, Glasgow, c.1890

3 - Wemyss Bay Railway Station Booking Office – where the roof fans out from the building like a great umbrella

4 - The War Memorial, 1927, opposite the Dick Institute in Kilmarnock, has similarities on a smaller scale to the Union Bank of Scotland Office

5

5 - Interior, Kirk of the Holy Rude, Stirling

6 - Canniesburn Hospital, Glasgow – an open-air hospital with emphasis upon light and air

7 - Skeldon House, Dalrymple, c.1780, overlooking the River Doon. Miller designed the neo-Georgian additions

8 - Kirk of the Holy Rude, Stirling – one of the country's finest medieval churches

6

7

8

1

1 - Sunlight Cottage – the only reminder of the 1901 Glasgow International Exhibition perched on a river bank near Glasgow University

2

2 - Elevations, Wemyss Bay Railway Station

3 - Porte cochère, Peebles Hydro

4 - Institution of Civil Engineers, Great George Street, Westminster, London

3

4

The **Anchor Line Building**, 12-16 St Vincent Place, Glasgow, 1905-7, however, designed for the Anchor Line Shipping Company, represents a distinct shift in style. A tall, seven-storey, steel-framed building, encased in brick, its façade is composed by a clearly defined plinth and attic, framing an entablature with a ghost of a triumphal arch at the centre. The simplicity is heightened by Miller's deployment of white faïence (glazed terracotta tiles – Carrara ware manufactured by Doulton).

Set against the Edwardian grime of the city centre, it was startlingly white and clean, reminiscent of the superstructure of the great liners that transported the company's passengers to the Mediterranean or across the Atlantic. It still contrasts wonderfully with the dark red sandstone façade and white clock faces on the tower of the T L Watson Bank of England building next door. Faïence was a costly, labour-intensive material, and detailed production drawings were required for each panel to take account of such problems as firing shrinkage. Although Miller's chief assistant, George Boswell, used it later at La Scala Cinema, Dundee, in 1913 (10), and Miller himself used it again for Cranston's Tearooms in 1915, in his subsequent commercial architecture he preferred white Portland stone.

The entrance is through a recessed portico at the centre, framed by Ionic columns which support a baroque pediment in nautical mode, with cherubs, and garlands of seaweed and seashells modelled by the great architectural artefact firm of H H Martyn of Cheltenham. The solid balcony at the second floor separates the lettable accommodation above from the company's offices on the lower floors. Interiors of marble and oak reflect the opulence of the first-class steamship saloons.

Miller had by now gained a good deal of experience with steel frames. The Anchor Line frame is cased in brick, and in situ concrete floor slabs are cast on to the joists, a system taken from the Chicago blocks at the end of the 19th century. (11) The façade, however, conveys nothing of this innovation in construction technique. It was only

Miller, not afraid to experiment, was the first Scottish architect to use faïence. (12) Its impervious nature was regarded as an innovation: *The surface cannot be affected either by smoke or chemically charged atmosphere; the material is in consequence highly adapted for buildings in manufacturing centres.* (13)

1 - Anchor Line Building, St Vincent Street, Glasgow

2 - Partick Fire Station, 120-124 Beith Street, Glasgow, 1906. A late Stuart design of brick and stone comprising 18 firemen's dwellings, an engine room for 5 tenders, a control room, staff rooms and a 40 metre tower for drying the hoses. It was converted into 23 flats and houses in 1988 by Simister Monaghan McKinney and Macdonald, later I H McKinney Architects

1

2

1 - Perspective, North British Locomotive Company Offices, Flemington Street, Springburn, Glasgow

2 - First-class dining saloon, SS Lusitania

after 1918, when Richard Gunn joined the practice, that Miller's commercial designs shed excess decoration to express the structure and function of the building more simply.

The luxury hotels of Peebles, Turnberry and Central Station, and his experience in steel construction, qualified Miller superbly for his appointment, in 1907, as consultant architect for the *Lusitania*, for Cunard. Miller assisted Robert Whyte, John Brown's in-house architect, in the design of its rich interiors. The resulting quality of the interior spaces demonstrated, at last, a complete fusion of engineering and architecture.

The artistic success of the architect is complete, because it is impossible to recognise the usual limitations in scope and execution involved in the case of a floating structure. (14) This comment referred to Miller's success in the design for the first-class dining saloon, a sumptuous, two-storeyed space focused upon an elliptical well, lit by a lavishly decorated dome 30 feet above. The decoration (as much elsewhere in Miller's work) was Louis XVI. Not all the diners on board were as architecturally pampered: regimented lines of tables stretched across the 1,200-seater third-class dining saloon as in the hall of any school. Upholstered chairs were replaced by wooden ones and no attempt was

3

Miller's design for the Prince of Wales Museum of Western India, 1907, was adjudged winner by the assessors, subject to approval by the Government of Bombay. The Government, however, rejected the design as the cost was considerably more than the amount prescribed. The assessors felt this objection was *outweighed by the importance of ensuring for Bombay a Museum of imposing appearance worthy alike of the important site it is to occupy and of the Royal personage whose name it is to bear.* **(15a) The commission was awarded to George Wittet, Bombay (1880-1926), second in the competition.**

4

made to conceal the structure, the only decoration of which was the fluted columns which marched across the room. Sadly, the Lusitania was torpedoed by the Germans on 7 May 1915, off Queenstown, Ireland, on its way to America. (15)

In 1907-8 Miller extended **Newark Castle**, Ayrshire, a 16th-century tower with fine views up the Clyde coast. Additions in 1687 and 1848-9 extended the tower into a Scottish baronial mansion, with steeply roofed tourelles, crow-stepped gables, dormer windows and an oriel window which opens out on to a corbelled projecting balcony supported upon two enormous brackets. The new wing accommodated a hall, smoking room, billiard room and library on the ground floor, and additional living accommodation above. Miller's extension remained within the language – crow-stepped gables, tiny pedimented windows breaking up the line of the eaves and a bay window echoing the oriel – of the original.

The **North British Locomotive Offices**, 110 Flemington Street, Springburn, Glasgow (now North Glasgow College) was Miller's next large commission. The plan was generated by a central courtyard clad in startling yellow and white faïence to reflect light into the surrounding rooms, but this bold use of a new material was kept firmly out

5

3 - Prince of Wales Museum of Western India, by George Wittet

4 - Interior, North British Locomotive Company Offices, Flemington Street, Springburn

5 - Elevation, Newark Castle extension, Ayrshire

1

2

3

1 - Interior, Institution of Civil Engineers, Great George Street, Westminster, London

2 - Institution of Civil Engineers

3 - Detail, Institution of Civil Engineers

of sight from the street. The principal façade is imposing three-storey baroque in red sandstone, with projecting end bays rising above the level of the attic, and giant aedicules framing deeply set windows. The sculpture on the flanking pilasters, less elaborate than that shown in Miller's original perspective, illustrates the engineering tools and instruments (eg. a governor for regulating the speed of an engine, a hammer and dividers). Some weird sculpture around the central door – notably a steam engine *with chains and haulage gear as swags* (16) set within a broken pediment – has been compared to *the surreal world of Magritte.* (17)

Flanking the entrance are figures representing *Speed* and *Science. Speed* holds an arrow in the direction of the wind blowing her cloak; *Science* sits on her globe, holding a torch in her left hand and a set of compasses in her right. Their function is symbolic, their only responsibility to grace the building and demonstrate the hopes and aspirations of the company. Their treatment is, therefore, lighter and more delicate than the untiring brawny figures supporting the balconies at the offices of the Caledonian Railway Company, Caledonian Chambers.

To undertake his London commissions, Miller worked from a temporary office in Victoria Street. He designed the extension to the Institution of Mechanical Engineers, directly across from the Institution of Civil Engineers, in comparable baroque.

In 1910 Miller won the competition for the **Institution of Civil Engineers**, Great George Street, Westminster, in limited competition with five other architects. Its immense two-storey baroque façade, finished in Portland stone (a material which Miller was to use in Glasgow twenty years later on Commercial Bank of Scotland, West Nile Street), is a powerful composition whose two slightly projecting wings frame an Ionic colonnade at first-floor level (*see p.C4*). The aedicules of these wings are set within arches, and support a sculptured ship's prow, complete with chains and paddles, similar to those of the interior of the Grand Central Dome at the Glasgow International Exhibition. Albert Hodge was the sculptor responsible for both. Over the entrance he modelled two boys to represent *Science* and *Engineering*, as support for the Institution's coat of arms. War postponed completion of the building, and the central panel of the ceiling of the great hall was painted by Charles Sims RA as a memorial to men killed in battle. (18)

The **Royal Infirmary**, **Perth**, begun in 1910 (with further alterations and additions throughout his career) was Miller's second hospital. Very different from the cramped site of Glasgow's Royal Infirmary was the greenfield site offered to Miller in Perth, on which he laid out a series of two-storey, brick and harl pavilions with hipped roofs and prominent chimneys. The windows are plain, and embellishment is restricted to the wings in the form of open-air balconies protected by a glass canopy as an extension of the hipped roof. The square towers topped with cupolas are a characteristic Miller motif.

4 - Entrance, Institution of Civil Engineers, Great George Street, Westminster, London

5 - Institutions of Civil and Mechanical Engineers, London

6 - Institution of Mechanical Engineers, Birdcage Walk, Westminster, London

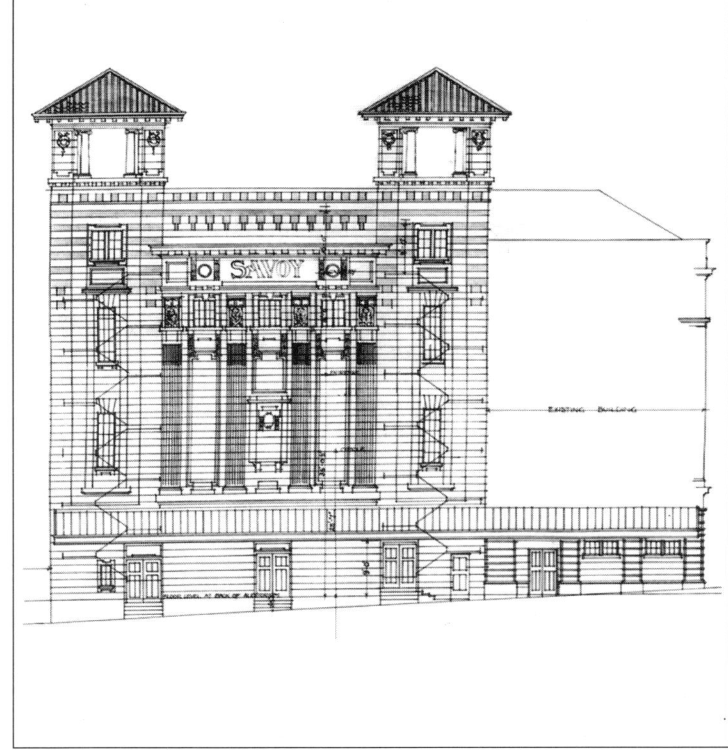

1

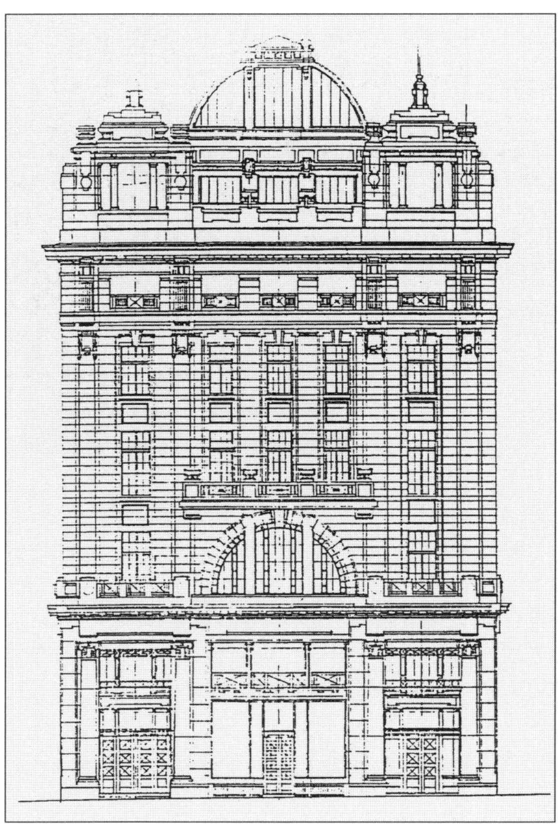

2

1 - **Front elevation, Savoy Theatre, Hope Street, Glasgow**

2 - **Front elevation, Cranston's Picture House and Tearoom, 13-15 Renfield Street, Glasgow**

There were few windows on the main elevation of the faïence-clad **Savoy Music Hall**, Hope Street, Glasgow, designed by Miller in 1911-12. Giant pilasters were used to articulate the elevation, which was framed by towers with broad-eaved pyramid roofs. The interiors were in the style of Louis XVI, *tastefully decorated, white and gold forming the predominant character in the scheme. A unique feature will be the tearoom adjoining the circle, and such an innovation should prove quite a boon, being the first time such a thing has been attempted in Glasgow.* (19) During the First World War it became known as the New Savoy Cinema; in 1958 the seats were taken out, the gallery, part of the balcony and the proscenium arches were removed, and it was converted into the Majestic Ballroom to sustain the latest dance craze. Closed in 1972, it was demolished (along with the Gaumont Cinema round the corner) to make way for the Savoy Centre.

The combination of tearoom and cinema provided a successful formula for **Cranston's Picture House and Tearoom**, 13-15 Renfield Street, Glasgow, 1914-16, built for Messrs Cranston's Tea Rooms Ltd on *one of the most prominent and valuable* [sites] *in the city of Glasgow.* (20) Miller again used white faïence cladding and the material, resembling marble, retained public favour: *it will be impervious to moisture, and will always retain its bright colour, and will form a conspicuous feature in the street architecture of the city.* (21) The six-storey beaux arts façade, characteristic of Miller's earlier classical work, reveals nothing of the structural contortions required to accommodate the large uninterrupted space of the cinema at first-floor level, which is sandwiched between more traditionally framed tearooms above and below. (22)

Interiors, designed by the one-time art nouveau designer, John Ednie, were in the style of Louis XVI, with a winter garden on the roof. They were reconstructed in 1935 by John McKissack. The building was bought over by the Classic Group, who used the building as a cinema until a fire damaged the interior in 1981. In 1990 it was refurbished and converted to offices by G D Lodge, Architects, who replaced the entire faïence façade, which had deteriorated considerably through time, with glass reinforced concrete.

Although the First World War seriously affected the construction industry, several large commissions kept Miller's practice going. In 1914 the Anchor Line commissioned a **store** at Yorkhill, Glasgow – a three-storey framed building, parallelogram in plan with its acute corners chamfered. The building is entirely functional, its structural grid interrupted only by a lift, two light wells and a corner staircase, and it represents a turning point in Miller's architecture. The construction was expressed to a much greater extent than before, and the fearless use of brick was an experiment for the rationalised neo-Georgian he favoured after the War. Large windows were articulated by red brick piers with concrete strips at floor level and a continuous band at roof level emphasising the horizontality. A subtle change in fenestration at the corners introduces a vertical intonation to terminate each elevation.

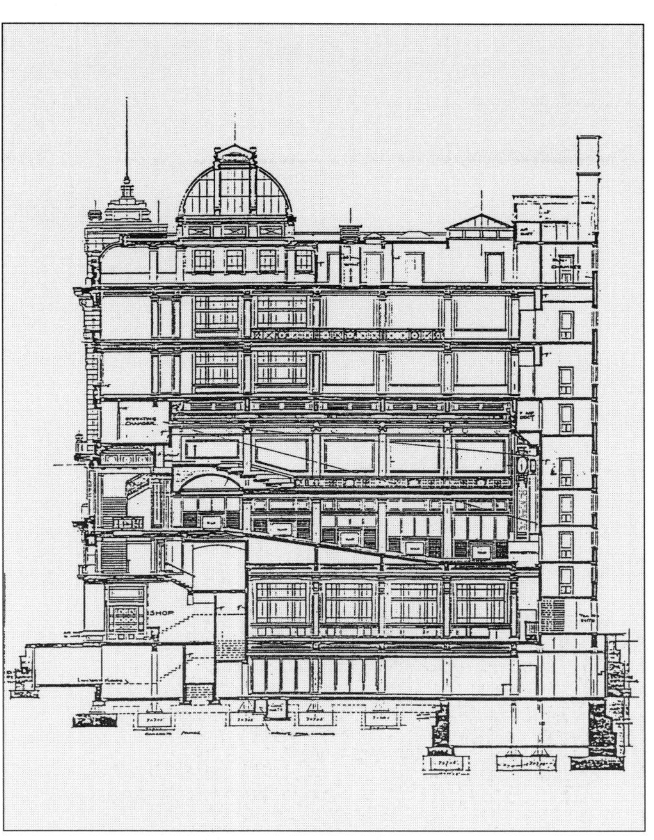

3

3 - Longitudinal section, Cranston's Picture House and Tearoom, 13-15 Renfield Street, Glasgow

James Miller 1915 – 29

1

2

3

Between 1915 and 1923 Miller designed the enormous **Kildonan** at Barrhill in Ayrshire for Captain David Euan Wallace MP, who married the daughter of Sir Edwin Lutyens in 1920. He designed the house before Wallace met Barbara Lutyens, but the coincidences of design are striking (*see p.C1*). Yet the backdrop of greenery softens the edges of the house and ties it to the landscape without resorting to the overgrown picturesqueness of some of its English counterparts. The culmination of the domestic architecture of Miller's early career, it approximates in size to the original plan for Turnberry Hotel, and has thus proved adaptable to several other uses – hotel, convent school and country club. There is a fine king-posted, roofed squash court, one of the first in the country. The manager of the hotel, who attended the convent school as a young girl, recalled a theatre, constructed as an adjunct.

Kildonan enjoys a challenging site, very restricted, bound by a river to the south, a burn to the west, and ground which rises steeply to the north and east. It stifles the architecture: *at close quarters the house suffers for want of an extensive lawn.* (1)

1 - Elevation, Kildonan, Barrhill, Ayrshire

2 - Kildonan

3 - Kildonan

4 

Miller's stately mansion is in the direct line of Lutyens' English Revival, with a romantic profusion of gables, bay windows and prominent clusters of chimneys piercing the Ayrshire skies. Individual details are simple and decoration is limited; it is the materials and the massing which create the grandeur. The 1928 *Architectural Review* attempted to capture its spirit: *the warm light creamy tone of the Northumberland sandstone with which the walls are built, and the rich brown grey colour of the large Caithness slates which cover the roof, are at one with Nature, chameleon-like in sunshine or shadow.* (2)

Windows have a distinctly horizontal emphasis (particularly on the west elevation), which ties the house firmly to the undulating landscape. The south façade is dominated by the two polygonal bay windows and the enormous square bay window of the main hall, whose glazing stretches up through both storeys to the eaves. The house was enormous – indeed too large for its owners.(3)

The stable block, with its white walls, hipped roof, and windows wrapping around the corners of the building, anticipates Miller's more adventurous architecture of the 1930s. The central, projecting arched entrance is surmounted by a clock tower.

During the War, and for several years after it, Miller designed a number of buildings, including the **Hydro** and **Hotel Majestic**, at Grange-over-Sands, and at St Anne's on Sea respectively, both popular holiday destinations for the Miller family.

During the 1920s and '30s Miller became renowned for large, American-influenced banks and commercial buildings in Glasgow's city centre, much of the work being attributable to his chief assistant, Richard Gunn.

The first of these is the handsome **McLaren Warehouse** (now Lomond House), 1922-4, on the corner of George Square and Hanover Street, for McLaren Sons & Company. Miller's belief that *a graphic or pictorial element* had to be added to any structural system characterises his approach to

Whether or not Miller visited any of Lutyens' buildings in the context of this commission, or was influenced by Christopher Hussey's championing of Lutyens in *Country Life*, the influence appears strong at Kildonan. Marsh Court, 1901-4, and Little Thakeham, 1902, were featured in *Country Life* in 1909, and the similarities between them and Kildonan are too great to be coincidental. Lutyens' internal spaces, minstrel galleries and carpentry seem present, and although it is much larger than Little Thakeham, there is a manifest resemblance in the relationship of roof forms and in the subtle modulation of otherwise flat elevations by the use of dormers, gables and bay windows. In stark contrast to the crumbly, picturesque Englishness of some of Lutyens' houses, and belying its detail, Kildonan stands stark, proud and geometric on the hillside.

4 - Interior, Little Thakeham, Sussex

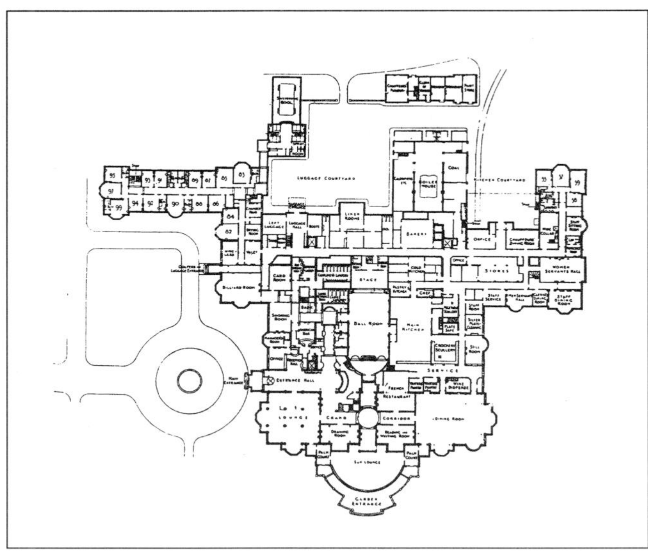
1

2

3

4

1 - The concept for the prestigious Gleneagles Hotel was formed by Miller & Matheson in 1913. War delayed construction after which Matthew Adam took responsibility for seeing the project through for the London Midland and Scottish Railway Company

2 - Perspective, Gleneagles Hotel, Perthshire

3 - Gleneagles Station was designed in 1919 by Miller and gave access to the hotel

4 - Gleneagles Station

the Warehouse. The eight-storey building is designed along the classical lines of major and minor axes of symmetry, in structural bays of an A B B C B B A rhythm on Hanover Street and A B B B C B B B A to George Square. Unfortunately, only the first phase of the building was constructed, producing a dissonant imbalance of A B B B C on the George Square façade. The vertical articulation of structure and glazing is interrupted by a deep band of horizontal stonework at second-floor level, capped by a mighty frieze and cornice. With the exception of the corners, where Miller cannot entirely dispense with classical treatment, the solidity is subordinate to the principal structural system, as in the work of Sullivan, Burnham and Root, and the Chicago School.

As the cast-metal spandrel panels serve no functional purpose, they become the principal decorative elements in the façade, although between design and construction Miller appears to have had second thoughts on decoration, for the stone balustrades, balconies and classical details at the frieze and cornice shown on the drawings were omitted in execution. A device inspired by Sullivan's Wainwright building is the roof-lit attic storey. The façade at attic level is a dominating expanse of solid masonry entablature forming a monumental termination to the series of identical floors below.

5

In 1920 James Miller carried out alterations to Randolphfield, Stirling, an 18th-century laird's house to which he added a stable block and extensive gardens.

6

Between 1922 and 1928 Miller supervised the removal of the 17th-century **Old West Kirk** in Greenock from Nicolson Street to Seafield to allow further shipyard expansion by Harland & Wolff. The knowledge which he thus derived of old structures was good training for his renovation of the Kirk of the Holy Rude, Stirling, some years later.

In 1923 he was commissioned to remodel 8-13 Blythswood Square, Glasgow, for the **Royal Scottish Automobile Club**. This terrace of four houses, designed in 1823-9 by William Burn and George Smith, forms the east flank of Glasgow's finest classical square, and was virtually identical to the other three sides. Miller had to convert terraced houses into a Club. At ground-floor level he created an opulent entrance hall and dining room, with a processional staircase leading to coffee rooms and other function suites, with a decor of French (beaux arts) inspired luxury. To the exterior he added mansard roofs and an entrance portico with fluted Ionic columns matching the original porticos and straddling the party wall between two houses. The rhythm of the windows at the first and second storeys betrays the anomaly otherwise neatly masked by a central coat of arms. (4)

7

8

5 - Randolphfield, Stirling

6 - McLaren Warehouse, George Square/Hanover Street, Glasgow

7 - Proposed addition, McLaren Warehouse

8 - Old West Kirk reconstruction, Seafield, Greenock

1

The **Richmond Memorial Hall** at Kirkoswald, 1923-5, which Miller designed for J R Richmond (a composition similar to his subsequent Forteviot Hall, 1925), is built of rubble beneath a big roof of Caithness slates, with a sweeping horizontality described as nautical (5), partly because the wall plane steps back at the upper level like a clerestory. The gable surges from this single-storey plinth to provide vertical punctuation, as does the clock above the pointed entrance door. The side elevations are pierced by four tall, hip-roofed, dormer-headed windows.

2

1 - Entrance hall, Royal Scottish Automobile Club, Blythswood Square, Glasgow

2 - Elevation, Royal Scottish Automobile Club

Forteviot's hall, although finished in harl with brick dressings and a red tile roof, is very similar, but there is more detail – a string-course and arched brick herringbone panels above the windows flanking the main entrance. The windows on the flanks are separated by raking buttresses which support the overhanging eaves. Miller had first been commissioned before the War to

3

Forteviot Village was commissioned by Lord Forteviot, who provided Miller with subsequent commissions later in his career in his capacity as chairman of Dewar's.

4

5

reconstruct Forteviot on the model of a garden city by Lord Forteviot of Dupplin, an old school friend from Perth Academy. In 1923 he revived the proposal, and between 1925 and 1927 ten houses, a village hall, a carpenter's shop and a smithy were constructed. The superseded village was then demolished. The ten houses are laid out in formal symmetry around a spacious central green, humanised by picturesque gables and dormers like Kildonan and Turnberry. The larger central gable signals a vennel to rear gardens at ground level. Timber trellises around the ground floor windows are appropriately mythological rustic.

3 - Forteviot Village Hall, Perthshire

4 - Elevation, Richmond Memorial Hall, Kirkoswald

5 - Forteviot Village Square

James Miller 1915 – 29

The type of design used in the Union Bank originated with McKim, Mead and White's reconstruction of Isaiah Rogers's Merchants Exchange, 1836-42, as the National City Bank, New York, 1904-10, in which Rogers's colonnade was retained as the lower half of the façade. (7)

1

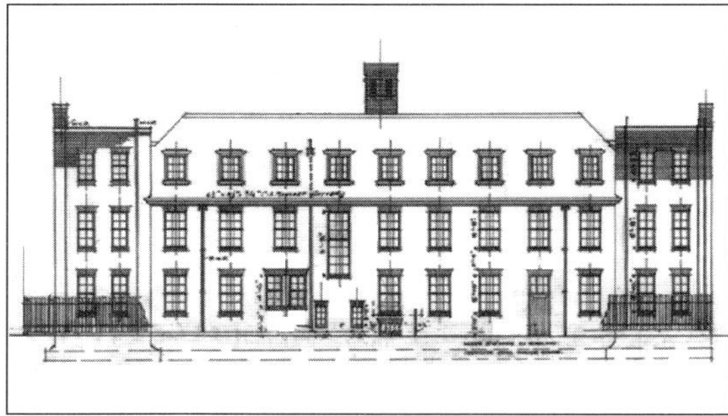

2

1 - Union Bank of Scotland Head Office, St Vincent Street, Glasgow

2 - Miller designed Princes Street House, Perth, 1923-4, as a hostel for the homeless commissioned by Lord Forteviot. English Late Stuart in style, it is built of red brick with stone dressings. The main entrance is enhanced with a segmental pediment and stone dressings

The majestic Head Office for the **Union Bank of Scotland**, now Bank of Scotland, 110-120 St Vincent Street, Glasgow, was won in competition in 1924. Miller was sufficiently proud of the design to submit it as his Diploma work for the Royal Scottish Academy upon election as an Academician in 1930. It represents a more confident handling of the separation of structure and infill, and most closely approaches the transatlantic classicism of, for example, the 1911 Chicago City Hall by Holabird and Roche. The deeply modelled Ionic order emphasises the supremacy of the structure over the set-back metal-framed glazed curtain walls. The design has a strength that recalls earlier Glaswegian architecture – the monumental designs of David Hamilton and James Sellars. The latter's 1873 St Andrews Halls has a similarly modelled treatment of the order.

In the *Architecture of Glasgow* Gomme and Walker too readily dismiss the design as plagiarism of York and Sawyer's 1913 Guaranty Trust building in New York, which was illustrated in the *Architectural Review USA* of the same year (6), since it is known that a copy had been lent by A G Lochhead to Richard Gunn, Miller's chief draughtsman and designer, in 1924 at the time of the competition.

3

The General Strike and a contractual dispute between Miller and his client impeded progress on the Union Bank. Miller and Gunn, considering that rosettes should be added to the entablature to bring the cornice and frieze into one, instructed Armitage to carry out the work without informing the Board of Directors. A letter of 23 June 1927 from Hird to Miller, objecting to the change, was probably reflective less of an interest in aesthetics than of the Board's annoyance at delays in construction – and of the fact that Gunn was overseeing the project rather than Miller himself.

4

Assumptions of plagiarism, however, oversimplify the position. Glaswegian architects were more freely experimental with American architectural theories than those elsewhere in Britain (eg. J J Burnet's 1911 Kodak Building in London, the design of which was developed by Thomas Tait).

That the Union Bank represents such a development in Miller's architecture may have been due to the influence of the client. Norman Hird, the Bank's Chairman, had visited America and Canada extensively during his study of American banking systems, and since York and Sawyer's Guaranty Trust building and Holabird and Roche's Chicago City Hall were the icons of capitalism at that time, it is probable that he visited them.

The floor area of the building was 108,228 sq ft comprising bank accommodation of 55,924 sq ft,

3 - Front elevation, Union Bank of Scotland Head Office, St Vincent Street, Glasgow

4 - Perspective, Union Bank of Scotland Head Office

1

1 - **Perspective, Dining Hall and open-air Tea Garden, Bournville**

lettable offices of 46,313 sq ft, shops 4,580 sq ft, and heating chamber 1,411 sq ft. The foundation stone of the Union Bank was laid by Viscount Novar KT in March 1926; but completion was reached only in December 1927, one month after it had been officially opened by the Prince of Wales and fully nine months after the original projected completion date. Yet the project did not run dramatically over budget: against the 1924 cost plan of £210,320 the final cost was £237,500.

Miller considered that *the architecture of the exterior should be an expression of its character and purpose.* (8) His design for the Union Bank, therefore, was a combination of imposing grandeur, transatlantic style and modernity. Enormous fluted columns take up the first three floors facing St Vincent Street (it was considered more inviting to bank customers if the base of the colonnade was brought down to street level). (9) The Greek detailing above is similar to that found above the

2

3

4

The chief factory extension, however, in recent years was the "Cocoa Block", completed in 1929, which, with its five storeys and 187,000 square feet of floor space, is the largest factory in the world devoted to this purpose. ... With its internal organisation and equipment, it can be claimed to be the last word as a plant for cocoa production. ... the principle of gravity-flow is adopted, by which raw material starts at the top of the building, passing through various processes from floor to floor by duct, pipe or chute.

Bournville Today, company newsletter

entrance to the McLaren Warehouse, crisp but rather faint, anticipating the more delicate decoration of later designs like the Commercial Bank of Scotland, West Nile Street and Troon Municipal Buildings. At the time, the Bank was regarded as *one of the finest buildings of its kind erected in this country within recent years.* (10)

During construction of the bank Miller was also designing a large neo-classical **Dining Hall** and a **Cocoa Block** for Cadbury's model town of Bournville. He combined the utilitarian language of a factory – brick, flat roof and large windows – with the luxury of a grand hotel with huge projecting wings, cornice and oriel windows. French windows enabled diners to spill out on to the terrace to catch some summer sunshine and melt.

2 - Dining Hall, Bournville

3 - Cocoa Block, Bournville

4 - Dining Hall, Bournville

1

2

3

1 - Perspective, Wyggeston Grammar School for Boys, Victoria Park Road, Leicester

2 - Main hall, Wyggeston Grammar School for Boys

3 - Entrance, Wyggeston Grammar School for Boys

In 1927 Miller was unsuccessful in his competition entry for Perth Academy, but successful in that for **Wyggeston Grammar School for Boys**, Victoria Park Road, Leicester. His scheme was selected from twenty-three entries because it was the *most simple, economical and straightforward design* (11) (comments remarkably similar to those for Glasgow University re the Natural Philosophy Building in 1904).

It is a pretty smart design, deploying large masses to the most effective result. Brick detail is limited to arches over the three main entrances, the largest in the centre. The two and three-storey pavilions are plain; countless windows march across the façades with unrelenting discipline, eased where the upper storey is stepped back to create some clerestory lighting. The central hall, with its large arched windows, anticipates Miller's design for Troon Municipal Buildings three years later.

Over three million bricks and 10,000 tons of cement were used in the construction of the **Stirling Royal Infirmary**, not far from his home at Randolphfield, which Miller designed in 1925. Opened on 10 August 1928 by the Duke and Duchess of York, the central pavilion is vaguely Lutyens: hipped swept roof, white pilasters punctuating the two-storey brick elevation, white window frames and tall chimneys. Regimented two-storey, concrete pavilions extend into the grounds with south-facing balconies at the ends to

5

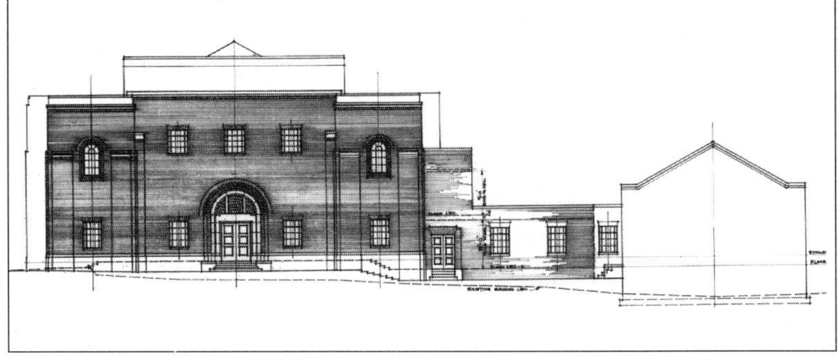

6

4

Mr James Miller ARSA, FRIBA, a Glasgow architect with a national reputation who has his home at Randolphfield, Stirling, was chosen by the Directors to prepare the plans for the new Infirmary in view of his experience in designing similar institutions in other parts of the country.

Royal Visit Pictorial Souvenir, 10th August 1928

offer patients the opportunity of fresh air to aid their recovery (a very inter-war preoccupation).

The **Woodhouse Warehouse**, 28-36 Renfield Street, Glasgow, now known as the Prudential Assurance Building, was designed in 1928 as a furniture warehouse for Mr Henry Levitt. Giant Ionic pilasters encompass the larger ground and first-floor windows, similar to the Union Bank of Scotland elevation (across the road), and a balcony runs across the length of the façade at second-floor level. Particular attention was paid to the fifth level, where the second and sixth bays have *oeil-de-boeuf* windows framed by swags beneath the giant cornice (*see p.C2*).

The sombre **Synagogue**, 4 Salisbury Road, Edinburgh, was built in 1929-32. Red brick Byzantine simplified into geometric form, it has a T-shaped plan. The familiar arch motif over a centrally positioned doorway is enlivened by a decorative panel. A large central dome, its structure supported by steel hangers which suspend it from the flat roof, flooded the raked seating below with light. The space was divided at gallery level in 1979 by Dick Peddie McKay. (12)

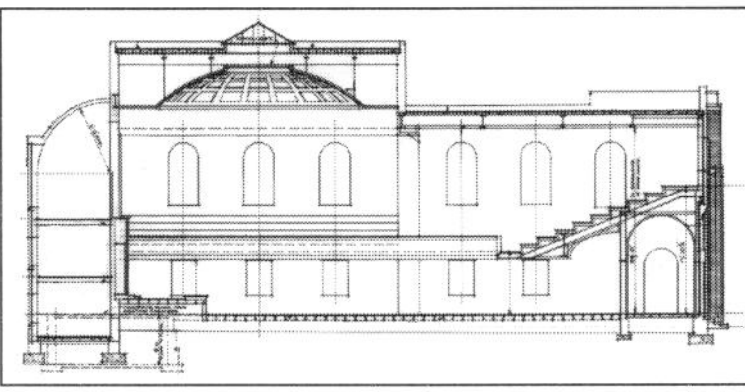

7

4 - Main pavilion, Stirling Royal Infirmary, Braehead, Stirling

5 - Elevation, Woodhouse Warehouse, Renfield Street, Glasgow

6 - Front elevation, Synagogue, Salisbury Road, Edinburgh

7 - Section, Synagogue

James Miller 1930 – 38

1

2

Miller was commissioned for Silver End, 1929-30, taking over from Thomas Tait and Frederick McManus of the J J Burnet practice. He built 90 flat-roofed modern-movement cottages and in so doing completed the modern housing begun by Tait/McManus. This work was so obviously in the style of Tait that it was previously attributed to him. (4)

1 - Troon Municipal Buildings, South Beach, Troon

2 - Academy Street elevation, Troon Municipal Buildings

By the 1930s Miller was in his seventies, an Academician of the Royal Scottish Academy, one of the Commissioners of the Royal Fine Art Commission for Scotland, and a member of the Scottish Architectural Advisory Committee of the Department of Health for Scotland. Such was his stature that Lord Weir proposed him as architect of St Andrew's House, Edinburgh (a commission eventually carried out by Thomas Tait). (1)

Miller's son George, who had attended the Glasgow School of Art and spent some years in Herbert Baker's office in London, returned to Scotland to join his father, taking over after the death of Richard Gunn in 1933. The name of the practice was changed to James Miller & Son. Little is known of how much George contributed to the practice, although the South African Pavilion at the 1938 Empire Exhibition is attributed personally to him. It may be presumed that the practice's increasing fondness for streamlining – *steamboat architecture* as the Swedes had it – was his.

Miller continued to favour a simplified English neo-Georgian for public buildings. The 1930-2 red brick **Concert Hall** and **Municipal Buildings** in **Troon** was built on a site gifted by one of Miller's earlier clients, Sir Alexander Walker. Miller had designed municipal buildings for the town back in 1915: a scheme grander in scale but postponed due to the war. (2) The 1930s scheme comprised council offices and a concert hall for 888 people built in red brick, with Blaxter stone dressings and *tiles of the Spanish 'roll' type ... a pleasing shade of reddish brown* on a hipped roof. (3) The entrance is defined by the projection of the central three bays, and highlighted by four giant, fluted, Composite pilasters, with delicately carved capitals, which rise through both storeys to an entablature crowned by a balustrade. The main door has a sturdy Roman Doric portico and French windows at first-floor level which open on to the balcony.

The **Commercial Bank of Scotland** on the corner of West Nile Street and West George Street, Glasgow, 1930-1, takes the Union Bank of Scotland design a step nearer Chicago. The punchy

3

5

strip of attic windows from the Union Bank has been removed, freeing the upper pilasters and allowing them to soar to the entablature. The power of this building lies in its vertical emphasis and bold use of white Portland stone upon a black granite plinth. Portland limestone had been considered for the exterior of the Union Bank, but dismissed as unsuitable for the polluted city centre. (5) So, by 1933 the fashion for pristine white buildings had begun to undermine pure *utility*. Decoration is minimal, incised in the latest neo-Egyptian style, with a frieze by Gilbert Bayes. More vertically expressive than the more solid Union Bank of 1924, although similar in brief, it is Miller's most striking design. Its most memorable feature, related to Miller's continuing interest in *utility* or functionalism, is where the glazed curtain wall of the upper floors to the lightwell is cantilevered beyond the line of the structure, in the manner developed on nearby Lion Chambers. Purely functional in expression, it continues a Glasgow tradition into the early 20th century.

4

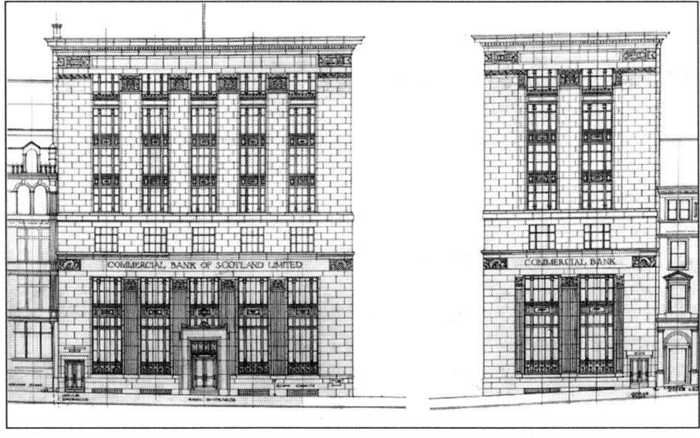

6

3 - Entrance, J & P Coats Building, St Vincent Street, Glasgow

4 - Elevation, J & P Coats Building

5 - Commercial Bank of Scotland, West Nile Street, Glasgow

6 - Elevations, Commercial Bank of Scotland

SCOTLAND'S FINEST ORGAN

HOLY RUDE CHURCH HAS IT VALUED AT £25,000

The Church of the Holy Rude congregation, Stirling, raised £27,000 of the £40,000 needed for the church restoration scheme. This was revealed by the Rev. Dr Lewis A. Sutherland, O.B.E., when addressing the Stirling branch of the National Council of Women at their luncheon meeting in McLachlan & Brown's restaurant, Murray Place, on Tuesday on the history of the Church of the Holy Rude.

"In fact," said Dr Sutherland amid laughter, "when the end of the restoration scheme came and the church was opened from end to end, I felt qualified to stand at any street corner with a tinny in front of me because the attitude of a mercenary had become almost my daily garment."

Dr Sutherland paid tribute not only to the generous donors of the money but to the architect, the late Mr James Millar, F.R.I.B.A., R.S.A., who, he said, was entitled to something like £1400 as his fee on a percentage basis of the cost involved but who point-blank refused to accept any money, thus making that great task of four and a half years' work a complete labour of love. Not only so, Mr Millar gave something like £300 to the fund. When he died in November, 1947, he was cremated and his ashes interred in the church in a casket with a suitable inscription on the wall.

The speaker said that the Church of the Holy Rude might be regarded as a Royal Church. It was the place of worship of kings and queens and it occupied the peculiar distinction of being the only Coronation Church in Scotland still standing and still being used for public worship. The other churches where kings and queens of Scotland were crowned were more or less in ruins. The

1

1 - Interior, Kirk of the Holy Rude restoration, Stirling

The tall, narrow, red sandstone **J & P Coats Building**, 155 St Vincent Street, Glasgow, 1931, was designed to a composition similar to that of the Woodhouse Warehouse. Only three bays wide, it has a base of giant Ionic pilasters. The unhappy collision between the entrance and the flanking pilasters is due partly to the restricted site.

In 1936 Miller was invited to re-unite the parts of the **Kirk of the Holy Rude** in Stirling, begun in 1456. After the Reformation it had been split up into three charges for three new parishes. Miller's task, which he undertook without remuneration (6), was to remove the later partitions and re-unify the Kirk. In doing so, he revealed the splendours of the crossing and the choir, thus restoring the Kirk to its rightful place as one of the country's finest medieval parish churches (*see p.C3*).

Just when Miller was about to produce one of his finest works – the Commercial Bank, Bothwell Street, in 1933 – his chief assistant, Richard Gunn, died. His untimely death does not detract from his significant influence on the firm's design. If his earlier buildings of the inter-war period display a

3

4

2

5

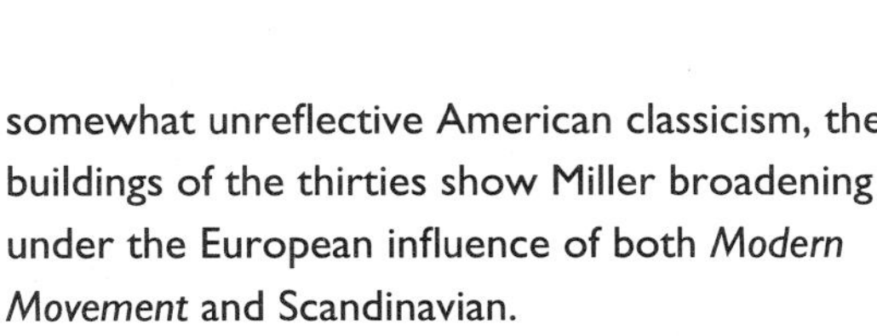

somewhat unreflective American classicism, the buildings of the thirties show Miller broadening under the European influence of both *Modern Movement* and Scandinavian.

The **Commercial Bank of Scotland**, 30 Bothwell Street, Glasgow, 1934-5, was the last of Miller's banks, a sturdy, authoritative, monumental building. Its Portland stone provides a stark contrast to the barely visible black plinth and the glass and iron curtain-wall set back behind the enormous Corinthian columns of the portico. Two rows of square windows punctuate the upper levels and, instead of a cornice, the top storey recedes very slightly. The Bothwell Street bank has

2 - Interior perspective, Kirk of the Holy Rude, restoration

3 - The Royal Visit to the Kirk of the Holy Rude, restoration, Stirling

4 - Commercial Bank of Scotland, Bothwell Street, Glasgow

5 - Kirk of the Holy Rude

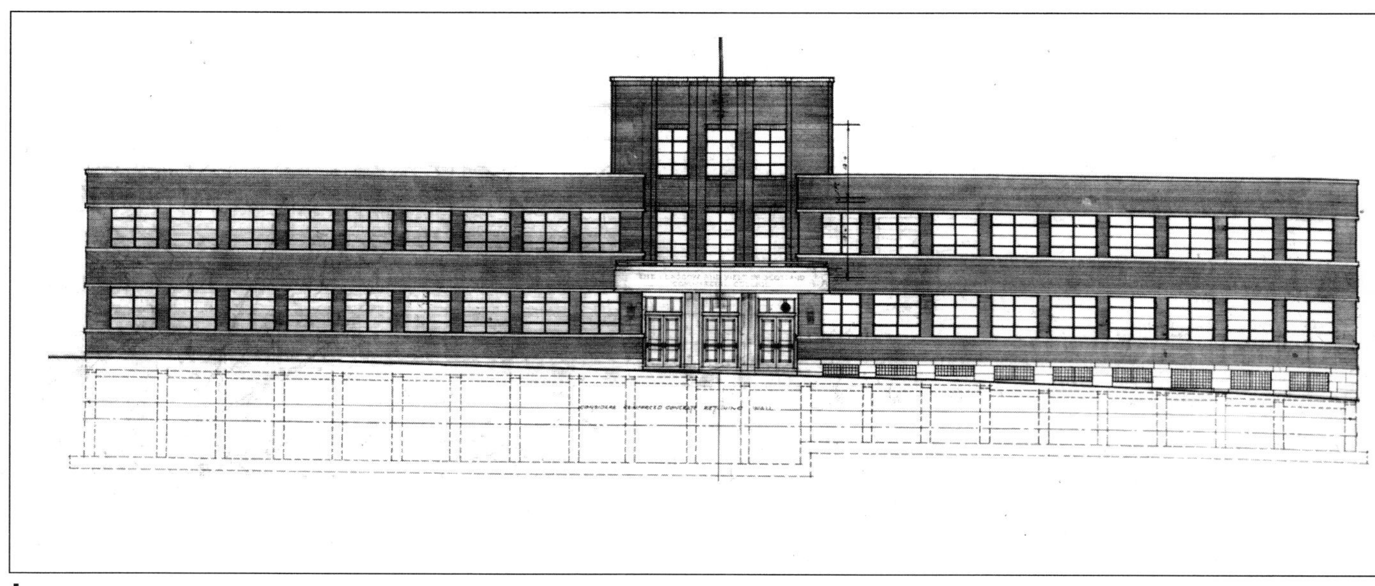

1

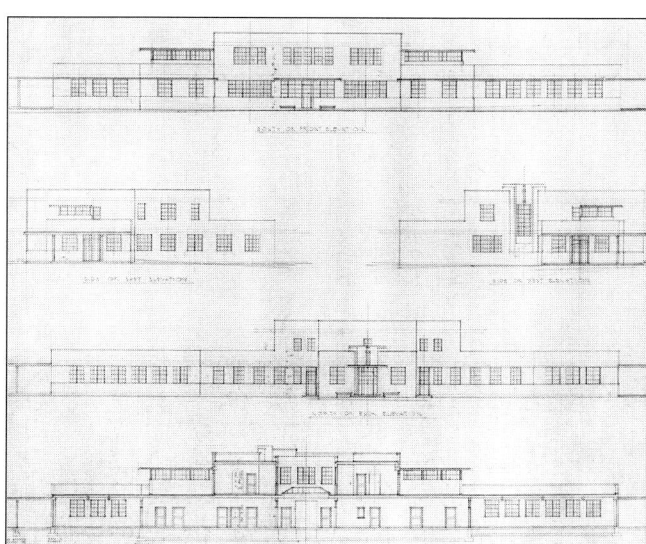

2

1 - Elevation, Glasgow & West of Scotland College of Commerce, Pitt Street, Glasgow

2 – The Royal Scottish National Institution, Larbert Colony, is more dynamic than Canniesburn with streamlined eaves shooting out from a low pavilion

a singular solidity, more conscious of the ground from which it rises than of the sky to which it aspires, for the originality lies in transforming what traditionally would have been a plinth into the entire composition (traces of Schinkel and Alexander Thomson's Egyptian revivalism). This sense of mass increases as the building rises, highlighted by the vertical strip windows and by the optical device of decreasing the window size above the cornice. An order is hinted at, in the side elevation, by fluted pilasters, although lacking a capital. The *frieze* is designed as alternating solid and void, with six panels carved by Joseph Armitage from an original design by Gilbert Bayes representing the six qualities of man in modern society – prudence, contentment, wisdom, justice, industry and commerce. (7) The bank not only breaks the rules of classicism but refines the hierarchical relationship between structure and cladding toward which Miller had been working for 20 years. A winged solar orb on the cast-iron panels was his concession to contemporary *Tutmania* – the craze for all things Egyptian.

The Bothwell Street bank was effectively Miller's last commercial commission and it marks the culmination of that strand of Glaswegian commercial architecture which had flowered from the mid-1890s until the war scares of 1938.

Estates Office,
Balmoral Castle,
Ballater.

9 September 1933

James Miller Esq., RSA, FRIBA,
15 Blythswood Square,
Glasgow

Dear Mr Miller,

Your plans and sketches for Birkhall have been duly submitted and both the King and Duke of York expressed appreciation of the way in which you have dealt with the somewhat difficult matter.

I am sorry to say, however, that His Majesty has decided to carry out no alterations at Birkhall for the present. The King has, however, directed that your plans should be retained so that if and when the alterations are to be carried out, the work should be in your hands.

I shall be greatly obliged if you ask your office in due course to forward me a note of your fees and expenses which have been incurred in the preparation of the plans, drawings and quotations.

Am I right in thinking that if the alterations were eventually undertaken you would make an allowance for the fees now due to be paid to you for the preparation of plans etc.

Believe me,
Yours very truly,

3

From about 1930 King George V lent Birkhall to the Duke and Duchess of York (later King George VI and Queen Elizabeth) who re-decorated it and planned the gardens. Situated on the Balmoral Estate above the river Muick, Birkhall is today used by Queen Elizabeth The Queen Mother.

Commercial architecture then entered a moribund phase from which it never recovered.

Miller thereafter cast the monumental American classical style from him, preferring long, low, buildings; an approach he adopted in the **Glasgow & West of Scotland College of Commerce**, Pitt Street, Glasgow, 1933 (now part of the headquarters of the Strathclyde Police). A bright red brick, three-storey block, streamlined by alternating prominent string-courses, its strong horizontal emphasis is ruptured in the middle: the central three bays are slightly recessed and vertical piers pull the eye to where the roof line is broken by a low tower. There is little to differentiate this building from the Anchor Line store at Yorkhill, twenty years before.

4

As assessor for the competition for the Infectious Diseases Hospital at Hawkhead, 1933, Miller had selected Thomas Tait as winner. Tait's approach was to inspire Miller's designs for Canniesburn Hospital and the Royal Scottish National Institution, Larbert, 1934. (8) **Canniesburn** was designed as an auxiliary hospital for the Glasgow Royal Infirmary, intended originally for private patients, those *of moderate means, between the hospital class of*

3 - Letter from Estates Office, Balmoral Castle, regarding Birkhall alterations

4 - Perspective, Canniesburn Hospital, Glasgow

1

patients and the well-to-do who can afford to go to private Nursing Homes. (9) The hospital was built on a 50-acre country site, half-way to Bearsden, gifted by Sir James McFarlane and his brother. It was an open-air hospital, with emphasis upon light and air. Patients experienced fresh clean air on the projecting balconies outside their ward, unlike the *hospital class* gulping in the filth and fumes of the city from their lofty promenade. The long, two-storey, brilliant white main pavilion was entered at the centre beneath a short tower (c.f. Pitt Street College) into a double-height brilliantly lit hall. Wings stretch out on either side, with a continuous terrace or balcony for each room or ward. Projecting circular staircases at each end are glazed in the fashionable manner (*see p.C3*).

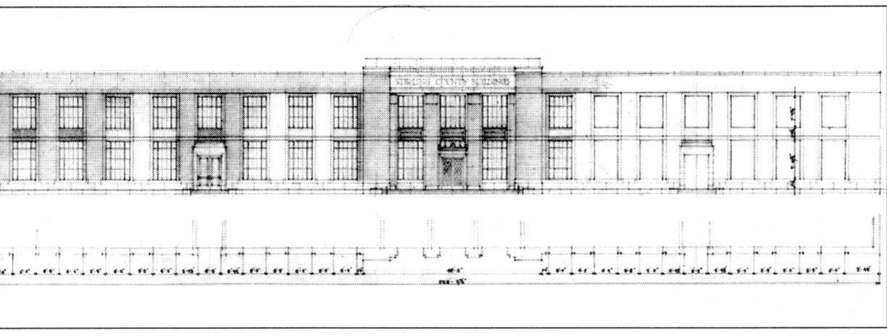

2

3

Stirling County Buildings, 1936-7, takes the neo-Georgian of Troon in the same direction: the same three central bays projecting from the main façade to emphasise the main entrance; the horizontally-proportioned windows were a sign of contemporary style.

The 1939 **Head office** for **Nairn Floors** in Kirkcaldy is the most distinguished of Miller's neo-classical '30s administration buildings, not least because of its beautiful stonework. In these buildings, as in his earlier banks, Miller redefined the classical language into an elegant, horizontally proportioned astylar building most closely approximated by his Royal Infirmary in Stirling.

1 - Balkissock House, Ballantrae

2 – Elevation, Stirling County Buildings, Stirling

3 – Nairn Head Offices, Kirkcaldy

4

5

The 1938 Empire Exhibition was a magnificent technical achievement, based upon Thomas Tait's construction method of steel and timber frames, with asbestos or timber panelling. Miller, now 78, did not form part of the inner core of designers, whose intention was to demonstrate the emergence of a new Scots architecture of strong geometry, and his buildings were largely peripheral, of no great moment beside the achievements of Tait, Spence, Marwick and Coia. The **South African Pavilion**, by Miller's son, George, was in the style of a farmhouse derived from the barns erected by the original Dutch settlers. It deployed the traditionally shaped gables – presumably at the request of his client. It was quite distinct from the modern pavilions around it, and attracted the comment: *in the wrong spirit but ... well carried out.* (10)

4 – South African Pavilion by George Miller, 1938 Empire Exhibition, Bellahouston Park, Glasgow as re-erected at Ardeer, near Ardrossan, Ayrshire

5 - The 1937 SMT Garage, Salkeld Street, 1937, attributed to James Miller, was built originally as the centre and stables for Glasgow's mounted police

1

In 1939 Miller designed the stately **Almond Lodge**, Cramond, Edinburgh, overlooking the golf course, for Mr & Mrs Henry J Levitt JP – the owners of the Woodhouse Warehouse. The two-storey house of weathered English brick and Portland stone has a hipped roof and prominent chimneys. Symmetry is found only at the rear where a central Doric porch projects creating a balcony for the French window above.

Envoi:

Sir Nikolaus Pevsner regarded James Miller's inter-war buildings as the ... *continuation of a Glasgow tradition rather than a revival inspired by the New York of McKim, Mead and White.* (11) Although not overtly designing within that Glasgow tradition, his architecture may be assessed as relevantly against the works of Alexander Thomson and James Sellars as against those of Norman Shaw and Lutyens, McKim, Sullivan and Holabird and Roche, whose details appear to have inspired him. His best work is taut, the language simple, and the detail continually honed to produce more from less. The origins of this approach may have lain in railway architecture, where minimalisation and utility of purpose in every detail produced some of the finest structures in the world.

All was subservient to Miller's conception of architecture as decorated structure, and his belief that structure should be the servant of client requirement. Only latterly was the architectural expression synthesised with the structure. Generally, it was selected for appropriateness. In his banks, Miller achieved his finest expression; imperatives fuse into significant architectural output.

1 - Almond Lodge, Cramond, Edinburgh

Notes & Bibliography

Introduction

(1) Oscar Wilde; *Essays and Lectures*, London (4th edition, 1913) p178
(2) Louis Sullivan; *Interstate Architect and Building 1901-1902*
(3) C F A Voysey; *Studio I*; p234
(4) Builder's Journal and Architectural Record, 12 March 1902
(5) Hermann Muthesius; *Das Englische Haus* (Berlin, 1904)
(6) C N Pevsner; *Pioneers of Modern Design* (1936) p159
(7) Builder's Journal and Architectural Record, op cit
(8) Mabel Harper, letter to RIAS
(9) RIAS obituary 1947
(10) Ibid

Chapter 1: 1888-1900

(1) Gordon Biddle and O S Nock; *The Railway Heritage of Britain: 150 Years of Railway Architecture and Engineering* (London: Joseph, 1983) p134
(2) Frank Wordsall; *The City that Disappeared: Glasgow's Demolished Architecture* (Glasgow: The Molendinar Press, 1981) p142
(3) Contemporary critics described the main industrial hall as an *Eastern Palace*. *The Exhibition Illustrated: a Pictorial Souvenir of the Glasgow International Exhibition* (Glasgow: The Scot's Pictorial Publishing Co, 1901) pp6,7
(4) Malcolm Higgs, Anne Riches, Elizabeth Williamson; *Buildings of Scotland: Glasgow* (Harmondsworth, Penguin, 1990) p334
(5) John Hume and Colin Johnston; *Glasgow Stations* (Newton Abbot: David and Charles, 1979) p128
(6) Alastair Alexander Gray; *Edwardian Architecture: A Biographical Dictionary* (London: Duckworth, 1985) pp348,348
(7) William Lyle; *Bridge of Weir* (Paisley: the author) 1975 pp31,32
(8) Perilla and Juliet Kinchin; *Glasgow's Great Exhibitions: 1988, 1901, 1911, 1938, 1988* (Wendlebury: White Cockade, 1988) p85

Chapter 2: 1901-14

(1) Higgs, Riches, Williamson; p209 op cit
(2) Hume, Johnson; p44 op cit
(3) Higgs, Riches, Williamson; p311 op cit
(4) John Patricia; *A Short History of Glasgow Royal Infirmary* (Glasgow) p30
(5) The Builder, Jan 12, 1901, p42
(6) Drawings in the RIAS Collection show early proposals for the hospital
(7) Higgs, Riches, Williamson; p341 op cit
(8) Minutes, Glasgow University
(9) Andor Gomme, David Walker; *Architecture of Glasgow* (London: Lund Humphries, John Smith & Son, 1968) p180
(10) Brian J Frew; The commercial architecture of James Miller: influences from Glasgow and abroad (unpublished dissertation, Glasgow School of Art, 1988)
(11) Frew; ibid
(12) Frew; ibid
(13) The Builder, June 29 1907, p787
(14) The Saloons of the Lusitania, Engineering, 19 July 1907, p68
(15) Des Hickey and Gus Smith; *Seven Days to Disaster: The sinking of the Lusitania* (London: Collins, 1981)
(15a) Records of the Prince of Wales museum of Western India
(16) Higgs, Riches, Williamson; op cit p438
(17) Frank Arneil Walker; *Glasgow: Phaidon Architectural Guide* (London: Phaidon, 1992) p116
(18) Garth Watson; *The Civils: the Story of the Institution of Civil Engineers* (London: Thomas Telford, 1988) p223
(19) *The Glasgow Programme*, 18 Dec 1911, p8
(20) Building Industries, 15 Aug 1914, p71
(21) Building Industries, ibid
(22) Frew; op cit

Chapter 3: 1915-29

(1) The Architectural Review, April 1928, vol 603, p127
(2) The Architectural Review, p124 ibid
(3) Rob Close; *Ayrshire & Arran: an Illustrated Architectural Guide* (Edinburgh: RIAS, 1992) p195
(4) Gomme, Walker; p78 op cit
(5) Rob Close, p173 op cit
(6) Gomme, Walker; p270 op cit
(7) Leland M Roth; *McKim Mead and White Architects*, p306
(8) James Miller; descriptive report on design submitted by James Miller ARSA for proposed new bank buildings at corner of St Vincent Street and Renfield Street, Glasgow, for the Union Bank of Scotland (Glasgow: unpublished, 2 June 1924) pp15-16: Frew op cit
(9) Frew op cit
(10) Architectural Review, April 1928, p124
(11) The Architect & Building News, 2 May 1929, p562
(12) John Gifford, Colin McWilliam, David Walker, Christopher Wilson; *The Buildings of Scotland: Edinburgh* (Harmondsworth: Penguin, 1984) p636

Chapter 4: 1930-38

(1) David Walker; *St Andrew's House: an Edinburgh Controversy* (Historic Buildings & Monuments, 1989) p27
(2) Ayrshire Post, 13 December 1929
(3) Ayrshire Post, 28 October 1932
(4) Research by Graham Thurgood:note in list of buildings at National Monument Record of Scotland
(5) Frew op cit
(6) Mrs Mabel Harper, notes
(7) Frew op cit
(8) Charles McKean; *The Scottish Thirties: an Architectural Introduction* (Edinburgh: Scottish Academic Press, 1987) p119
(9) John Patricia; p37 op cit
(10) J M Richards; Glasgow 1938: A Critical Survey (Architectural Review, July 1938) p6
(11) C N Pevsner op cit

Academy Architecture; Architectural Heritage Archives of the University of Strathclyde; The Architect; Architect and Building News; Architect's Journal; Architecture Illustrated; Architectural Review; Ayr Advertiser; Ayrshire Post; The Bailie; Bell Colin & Rose, **City Fathers: the Early History of Town Planning in Britain**. London: Barrie & Rockliff, The Cresset Press, 1969; Biddle, Gordon & Nock, OS, **The Railway Heritage of Britain: 150 Years of Railway Architecture and Engineering.** London: Joseph, 1983; Binney, Marcus & Pearce, David, **Railway Architecture**. London, Orbis Books, 1979; Brinnin, John Malcolm, **The Sway of the Grand Saloon**. London: Arlington, c.1971; Brown, John, **Clydebank in Old Picture Postcards**. Zaltbommel: European Library, 1985; The Builder; Builder's Journal and Architectural Record; Builder's Journal and Architectural Engineer; Building Industries; Carris, Nicholas, Thomas, **North Atlantic Passenger Liners since 1900**, Shepperton: Allan, 1972; Clydebank and Renfield Press; Cooper, Nicholas and Lemere, H Bedford, **The Opulent Eye: Late Victorian and Edwardian Taste in Interior Design**. London: Architectural Press, 1976; Council Minutes, Clydebank; Country Life; Dean of Guild Plans, Strathclyde Regional Archives, Kyle & Carrick; Doak, A M and Andrew McLaren Young, **Glasgow at a Glance: An Architectural Handbook**. Glasgow: Collins, 1971; London: Hale, 1977; **Empire Exhibition Scotland Souvenir**, Glasgow, 1938; Engineering; The Entertainer; Eyre-Todd, George, **Who's Who in Glasgow in 1909**, Glasgow and London, 1909; **Exhibition Illustrated: A Pictorial Souvenir of the Glasgow International Exhibition**, the Scot's Pictorial Publishing Company Ltd, Glasgow, 1901; Frew, Brian J, **The commercial architecture of James Miller: influences from Glasgow and abroad**. unpublished dissertation, Mackintosh School of Architecture, 1988; Gifford, John; McWilliam, Colin; Walker, David; Wilson, Christopher; **The Buildings of Scotland: Edinburgh**, Harmondsworth: Penguin, 1984; Glasgow Advertiser and Property Circular; Glasgow Contemporaries, 1901; Glasgow Herald; The Glasgow Programme; **Glasgow Royal Infirmary, Highlights of its History**. Matt Macdonald, Glasgow; Gomme, Andor and Walker, David, **The Architecture of Glasgow**. London: Lund Humphries, 1968, 1987; Govan Press; Gray, Alexander Stuart, **Edwardian Architecture: A Biographical Dictionary**. London: Duckworth, 1985; Hanley, Cliff ed. **Glasgow: A Celebration**. Mainstream Publishing, Edinburgh, 1984; Hannay, John, **The Glasgow Domestic Architecture of James Miller**, unpublished dissertation, Mackintosh School of Art Library; Hay, Marianne H, **Glasgow Theatres and Music Halls: A Guide**, Glasgow: Mitchell Library, 1980; Hickey, Des and Smith, Gus, **Seven Days to Disaster: The Sinking of the Lusitania**. London: Collins, 1981; **History of the University of Glasgow**, Glasgow, 1909; Howson L D, **Central Station: an architectural and historical study**. unpublished dissertation, Mackintosh School of Art, 1977; Hume, John and Moss, Michael, **Glasgow as it was vol. II: Sports and Pastimes**. Nelson: Hendon, 1975; Hume, John R and Johnston, Colin, **Glasgow Stations**. Newton Abbot: David and Charles, 1979; Kenna, Rudolph, **Glasgow Art Deco**. Glasgow: Drew, 1985; Kinchin, Perilla and Juliet, **Glasgow's Great Exhibitions: 1888, 1901, 1911, 1938, 1988**. Wendlebury: White Cockade, 1988; Larmour, Paul, **Belfast: an Illustrated Architectural Guide**. Belfast: Friar's Bush Press, 1987; Louden, T, **The Cinemas of Cinema City** (sl):(sn), 1983; Lyle, William H, **Bridge of Weir**. Paisley: (the author), 1975; McBain, Janet, **Pictures Past: Recollection of Scottish Cinemas and Cinema-going**. Edinburgh: Moorfoot, 1985; McKean, Charles , **Edinburgh: an Illustrated Architectural Guide**. Edinburgh: RIAS, 1982; McKean, Charles; Walker, David; Walker, Frank, **Central Glasgow: an Illustrated Architectural Guide**. Edinburgh: Mainstream Publishing and RIAS, 1989; McKean, Charles, **The Scottish Thirties: an Architectural Introduction**. Edinburgh: Scottish Academic Press, 1987; McKean, Charles, **Stirling and the Trossachs**. Edinburgh: RIAS and Scottish Academic Press, Edinburgh, c.1985; Meldrum, Neil, **Forteviot: the History of Strathearn Parish**. Paisley: Alexander Gardener, 1926; Morton, Henry Brougham, ed. **A Hillhead Album**. Glasgow: Glasgow University Press, 1973; Muthesius, Hermann, **The English House**. Berlin: Wasmith, 1904 London: Crosby Lockwood Staples, 1979; Nicoll, James, **Domestic Architecture in Scotland**. Aberdeen: Daily Journal Offices, 1908; Oakley, C A, **The Second City: the Story of Glasgow**. Glasgow and London: Blackie, 1990; **Official Souvenir Handbook, The Royal Visit in connection with the opening of the New Infirmary, Perth**. Perth: J McKinley, 10 July, 1914; Patricia, John, **A Short History of Glasgow Royal Infirmary**. Glasgow; Perth Royal Infirmary, annual report; Perthshire Advertiser; Pevsner, Nikolaus **Leicestershire and Rutland**. Harmondsworth: Penguin, 1960 (1984); Pevsner, Nikolaus, **The Buildings of England: The Cities of London and Westminster**. Harmondsworth: Penguin, 1973; Post Office Directories; RCAHMS; Register of listed buildings, SDD; Reid, Rev Andrew, David B Taylor ed. **The Parish of Forteviot** in the 3rd Statistical Account of Scotland v.27 Cupar, Angus: Culross, 1979; Richards, J M, ed. **Who's Who in Architecture: 1914:** London: Weidenfield and Nicholson, 1977; RIAS Drawings Collection; RIAS Quarterly Illustrated; RIBA Journal; RMS *Lusitania* and *Mauretania*, Coronation Booklet 1911, (Edition de luxe), the Cunard Steamship Company Ltd; Royal Fine Art Commission for Scotland, minutes; Royal Scottish Academy Exhibition Catalogue, 1826-1916, 1917-77; Royal Scottish Academy annual reports 1941-75; Royal visit to Stirling, Official Souvenir Programme; Scottish Field; Service, Alastair, **Edwardian Architecture: A Handbook to Building Design in Britain, 1890-1914**. London: Thomas and Hudson, 1977; Service, Alastair, ed. **Edwardian Architecture and its Origins**. London: Architectural Press, 1975; Service, Alastair, **Edwardian Interiors: Inside the Homes of the Poor, the Average and the Wealthy**. London: Barrie and Jenkins, 1982; Simpson, W, Douglas, **The Church of the Holy Rude, Stirling: history and guide book**. Society of Friends of the Church of Holy Rude, 1967; Simpson, William, revised by A H Millar, **Glasgow in the Forties**, 1889; Sinclair, Fiona, **Scotstyle**, Edinburgh: RIAS, 1984; Skillen, Brian, **Glasgow on the Move**, Glasgow: Glasgow District Libraries, 1984; Stephenson Locomotive Society, **The Glasgow and South Western Railway 1850-1923**. London: Stephenson Locomotive Society, 1950; Stevenson, J B, **Exploring Scotland's Heritage: The Clyde Estuary and Central Region**. Edinburgh: RCAHMS, HMSO, 1985; Stirling Journal and Advertiser; Troon Primary School Records; Walker, David, **St Andrew's House: an Edinburgh Controversy**. Historic Buildings & Monuments, 1989; Walker, Frank Arneil, **Glasgow: Phaidon Architectural Guide**. London: Phaidon, 1992; Walker, Frank Arneil, **The South Clyde Estuary**. Edinburgh: Scottish Academic Press, 1986; Watson, Garth, **The Civils: the Story of the Institution of Civil Engineers**. London: Thomas Telford, 1988; Williamson, Elizabeth; Riches, Anne; Higgs, Malcolm, **The Buildings of Scotland: Glasgow**. Harmondsworth: Penguin, National Trust for Scotland 1990; Worsdall, Frank, **The City that Disappeared: Glasgow's Demolished Architecture**. Glasgow: The Molendinar Press, 1981; Worsdall, Frank, **Victorian City**. Glasgow: Drew, 1988

Chronology

1889-90	Bridge Street Railway Station, Glasgow
1889	Fort Matilda Railway Station, Greenock
1889	Gourock Pier Railway Station (partially demolished)
1889	Greenock West Railway Station
c.1890	Craighuchty Terrace, Aberfoyle
1890	Dunloskin, Dumbreck, Glasgow
1892	Ardlonish, 30 Sutherland Avenue, Pollokshields, Glasgow
1892-4	Belmont Parish Church, 121 Great George Street, Hillhead, Glasgow (now Laurel Bank School assembly and dining hall)
1892	Troon Railway Station
1893-1902	Clydebank Municipal Buildings, Dumbarton Road, Clydebank (complex comprising municipal offices, town hall (including lesser hall), police department, public baths, fire station (with firemen's dwellings) and library
1893	Princes Pier Railway Station, Greenock (demolished)
1893-4	St Mary's Episcopal Church, Aberfoyle
1894	Stations on West Highland Railway (attributed to Miller): Ardlui, Arrochar & Tarbet, Bridge of Orchy, Crianlarich Upper, Fort William, Rannoch, Spean Bridge, Whiteinch, Yoker Ferry
1896	Botanic Gardens Station and Entrance Lodges to Botanic Gardens, Great Western Road, Hillhead, Glasgow (station demolished following fire)
1896	Bowling Railway Station
1896	Coatbridge Central Railway Station
1896	Dumbarton Central Railway Station
1896	Dumbarton East Railway Station
1896	Kelvinbridge Railway Station, Caledonian Crescent, Kelvinbridge, Glasgow (demolished)
1896	Kilbowie Railway Station
1896	Old Kilpatrick Railway Station
1896	St Enoch Underground Station, St Enoch Square, Glasgow
1896	Scotstoun East Railway Station
1896	Scotstoun West Railway Station
1897	Belfast City Hall competition entry (not built)
1897	1-8 Caledonian Mansions, 445-459 Great Western Road, Kelvinbridge, Glasgow
1898-1901	Glasgow International Exhibition, Kelvingrove Park, Glasgow
1898	2 Lancaster Crescent, Kelvinside, Glasgow
1898	St Columba's Episcopal Church, Baltic Street, Bridgeton, Glasgow
1898	Shops alterations, 265-267 Sauchiehall Street, Glasgow
1898	Tenement, Norfolk Street, Gorbals, Glasgow
1899	Alterations and additions, 10 Windsor Terrace, Glasgow
1899-1906	Central Railway Station extension, Hope Street, Glasgow
c.1899	Cove Bay Railway Station
1899-1900	Linthouse St Kenneth Free Church, 7-9 Skipness Drive, Govan
1899	Shop alterations, 140 Douglas Street, Glasgow
c.1900	Additions, Auchenflower, Ballantrae
1900	Adelphi Hairworks, alterations and additions to central building, Govan Street, Glasgow
1900	Alterations and additions, 5 Devonshire Gardens, Kelvinside, Glasgow
c.1900	137 Bentinck Drive, Troon, for Sir Alexander Walker
c.1900	Coupar Grange House, gardens and cottage, Bendochy Parish, Perthshire
1900	Lintwhite School, Lintwhite Crescent, Bridge of Weir
1900	Performing Animals Shelter, 326-328 Sauchiehall Street, Glasgow
c.1900	1 Princes Terrace, Dowanside, Glasgow
1900	West Kilbride Railway Station
1900	10 Lowther Terrace, Kelvinside, Glasgow (later additions 1904 and 1909)
1901-3	Caledonian Chambers, 75-97 Union Street, Glasgow
1901	Cambusnethan Railway Station
1901	Doune Railway Station
1901-7	Glasgow Royal Infirmary, reconstruction, 106 Castle Street, Glasgow
c.1901	Mauchline Railway Station
1901	Office and warehouse, alterations, 26-30 Jamaica Street, Glasgow
c.1901	Prestwick Railway Station
1901	Ranfurly Hotel, extension, Castle Terrace, Bridge of Weir
1901	Shop, alterations, 116 & 120 Union Street, Glasgow
c.1901	Stevenston Central Railway Station
1901	Theatre Royal, alterations, Hope Street, Glasgow
1902	Villa, Tullylumb Terrace, Perth
1902-4	MacGregor Memorial Church, 139 Crossloan & 1 Craigton Road, Govan, Glasgow
1903	Appin Railway Station
1903	Ardrossan North Railway Station
1903	Ballachulish Railway Station (Glencoe)
1903	Benderloch Railway Station
1903	Burnside Railway Station
1903	Creagan Railway Station
1903	Duror Railway Station
1903	Kentallen Railway Station
1903	Kirkhill Railway Station
1903	Lugton Railway Station
1903	Muirend Railway Station
1903	Newton Railway Station
1903	Neilston Railway Station
1903	Patterton Railway Station
1903	Alterations to shops, 218/220 Sauchiehall Street, Glasgow
1903	South Stand, Hampden Park football ground, Mount Florida, Glasgow
1903	Uplawmoor Station
1903	Offices (Olympic House), George Square and Queen Street, Glasgow
1903-4	Wemyss Bay Railway Station and cottages
1903	Whitecraigs Railway Station
1903-7	Materia Medica & Physiology Buildings, Glasgow University, Glasgow
1903-6	Natural Philosophy Buildings, Glasgow University, Glasgow
1903-4	8 Lowther Terrace, Kelvinside, Glasgow
1903-4	St Andrew's East Church, 681-685 Alexandra Parade, Dennistoun, Glasgow
1904	Alterations and additions, Brampton House, 160 Camphill Avenue, Mount Florida, Glasgow
1904-5	Jordanhill Parish Church, 28 Woodend Drive, Jordanhill, Glasgow
1904-7	Turnberry Hotel & Railway Station, Turnberry
1905-7	Peebles Hydropathic Hotel, reconstruction, Peebles
1905	Drumchapel School, Drumchapel, Glasgow (design, from 1901 exhibition, possibly by Miller)
1905-6	Garden City, Dalmuir and Kilbowie for Sir Robert McAlpine
1905-7	Anchor Line Building, 12/14/16 St Vincent Place, Glasgow
1906	Sir John Neilson Cuthbertson School, Cuthbertson Street & Coplaw Street, Pollokshields, Glasgow
1906-7	SS Lusitania, interiors (with A McInnes Gardner)
1906	Partick Fire Station, 120-4 Beith Street, Partick, Glasgow
1907	Central Station Hotel, extension, 71-99 Gordon Street, 30 Hope Street, Glasgow
1907	Automobile Owners Ltd, Lancefield Street, Glasgow
1907-8	Newark Castle, additions, Ayrshire
1908	Nodesdale House, Largs
c.1908	Lodge, Alexandra Public Park, Sannox Gardens, Dennistoun, Glasgow
1908	Fullerton Public School, Burnside Place, Troon
1908	Prince of Wales Museum of Western India, (unexecuted)
1908	Skeldon House, alterations and additions, Dalrymple, Ayrshire
1908	Gask House, Perthshire
1908-9	North British Locomotive Company offices, 110 Flemington Street, Springburn (now North Glasgow College)
1909	Dunholm, 76 Hamilton Avenue/Springkell Avenue, Pollokshields, Glasgow
1910	Blackwood Railway Station
1910-13	Institution of Civil Engineers, Great George Street, Westminster, London
1910	Larkhall Central Railway Station
1910	Laurencekirk Railway Station
1910	Lesmahagow Railway Station
1910	Monktonhead House, Monkton, Ayrshire
c.1910	Slateford Railway Station

1910 Stonehouse Railway Station
c.1910 Strathaven Central Railway Station
1911 New Central Dispensary, 30 Richmond Street, Glasgow
c.1911 Institution of Mechanical Engineers, Birdcage Walk, London
1911 Perth New Infirmary, Taymount Terrace, Perth (later additions: 1912, 1914, 1922, 1924, 1926, 1928, 1929, 1931, 1933, 1938)
1911 Savoy Theatre, 371 Hope Street, Glasgow (now demolished, replaced by the Savoy Centre)
1912-15 Stirling Railway Station
1912 House, Bridge of Weir
1913 Tollcross Tube Works, 1300 Tollcross Road, Glasgow
1913 Alterations, Buchanan Street/Renfrew Street, Glasgow
1913 Gleneagles Hotel (constructed 1919 by Matthew Adam)
1913-14 Blanefield House, Kirkoswald, Ayrshire
1913 Laggan House, extension, Ballantrae
1914 Atholl Palace Hotel, alterations and additions, Pitlochry
1914-16 Cranston's Picture House and Tearoom, 13-15 Renfield Street, Glasgow
1914 Rowantreehill villa, additions, Rowantreehill Road, Kilmalcolm
1915 Scottish Filling Factory, Georgetown
1915 Palace Hotel, alterations, Aberdeen
1915 Alterations and additions, Imperial Hydropathic Hotel, St Anne's on Sea
1915-23 Kildonan House, garage, stables and two houses, Barrhill, Ayrshire
1919 Benbow Hotel, Dalmuir
1919 Workmen's Houses, Rushcliffe Halt, Hill Farm, East Leake, Nottinghamshire
1919 Gleneagles Railway Station, Gleneagles
1920 Randolphfield, alterations and additions, Stirling
1920 Washhouse, toolhouse and verandah, 4 St Leonard's Bank, Perth
c.1920 Pitheavlis cottages (possibly Miller), Low Road, Perth
1920 Alterations, The Royal Hotel, Bridge of Allan
1920-4 Hazelwood Hydropathic establishment, alterations, Grange over Sands
c.1920 High Blantyre Railway Station
1921 Banastre Holm, St Anne's on Sea
1921 Hotel Majestic, St Anne's on Sea
1921 William Lochead's Trust, alterations, Union Street, Glasgow
1922 War Memorial, Barbieston Road, Dalrymple
1922-8 Old West Kirk, reconstruction, Seafield, Greenock
1923 The Royal Scottish Automobile Club, remodelling, 8-13 Blythswood Square, Glasgow
1923 Barrhill District War Memorial Hall, Barrhill
1923 McLaren Warehouse, George Square/5 Hanover Street, Glasgow (now Lomond House)
1923-4 Lodging House, (hostel for the homeless), 55 Princes Street, Perth (pram shed added in 1925) for Lord Forteviot
1923-9 Houses, Gleneagles
1924 Aultwharrie, Dunblane
1924-5 Dalblair Hotel, alterations, Alloway Street, Ayr
1924 Garage reconstruction, Eastwood Park
1924 Gartcosh Railway Station
1924 Glenboig Railway Station
c.1924 Kirtlebridge Railway Station
1925 Addiewell Railway Station
1925 Bellshill Railway Station
c.1925 Carluke Railway Station
1925 Memorial Hall, Kirkoswald, Ayrshire
1925 Drill Hall, alterations, Yorkhill Street, Glasgow
1925 House, Kildalloic, Campbeltown
1925 Glenrinnes, alterations and additions, Dufftown
1924-7 Union Bank of Scotland Head Office, 110/120 St Vincent Street, and 29-36 Renfield Street, Glasgow
1925-6 Forteviot Village reconstruction
1926 Kilmarnock Agricultural Hall, reconstruction, Kilmarnock
1926 War Memorial, Elmbank Avenue, Kilmarnock
1926-8 Stirling Royal Infirmary, Braehead, Stirling
1927 Dining Hall, Open Air Tea Garden and Cocoa Block, Bournville
1927 Perth Academy competition entry (unbuilt)
1927-9 Wyggeston Grammar School for Boys, Victoria Park Road, Leicester
1928 Woodhouse Warehouse, 28-36 Renfield Street, Glasgow (now Prudential)
1928-9 Administration Building, alterations and additions, Cathcart
1928 Cherrybank Cottages, Perth
c.1928 Dupplin Castle East Lodge, near Forteviot
1929-32 Synagogue, 4 Salisbury Road, Edinburgh
1929 Houses, Silver End, Essex
1929 Alterations, 53 Kent Road, Glasgow
1930-2 Municipal Buildings, South Beach, Troon
1930 Crutherland, alterations and additions, East Kilbride
1930 Dankeith House, alterations and additions, Kilmarnock
1930 Dewar's Bottling and case making warehouses, Glasgow Road and Glover Street, Perth (further additions 1932)
1930 Commercial Bank of Scotland, 92-98 West George Street/West Nile Street, Glasgow (now Royal Bank of Scotland)
1930-4 National Commercial Bank, 30 Bothwell Street and 100 Wellington Street, Glasgow (now Royal Bank of Scotland)
1931 Proposed demolition/new offices, York Place, Perth (not proceeded with)
1931 Stirling County Buildings, Viewforth House, Stirling
1931 Perth County Buildings, York Place, Perth
1931 J & P Coats Building, 155-157 St Vincent Street, Glasgow
1931 Station Hotel, alterations and additions, Stirling
1932 Roof over railway siding, Dewar's Distillers, Glasgow Road
1933 Glasgow & West of Scotland College of Commerce, 173 Pitt Street, Glasgow
1933 Alterations, West George Street, Glasgow
1933 Balkissock House, Ballantrae
1933 Birkhall, alterations (unexecuted) for H M
1934 Airthrey Paper Mills, Bridge of Allan
1934 Marr College, Sports Pavilion, Dundonald Road, Troon
1934 The Royal Scottish National Institution, Larbert Colony
1934 Squash Rackets Club, Maryhill, Glasgow
1934 Air Raid Shelters, Broomloan Road, Ibrox, Glasgow
1934 House, Barstobrick
1935 Simpson Memorial Maternity Pavilion, Royal Infirmary, Edinburgh (Miller as consultant)
1935 Stow College, Cowcaddens, Glasgow
1935 Canniesburn Hospital & Convalescent Homes, Canniesburn, Glasgow
1935 Achnashellach Lodge, alterations, Ross-shire
1936 Wigtown Lodge, alterations, Galloway, Garlieston
1936 Broadcasting House, additions, Queen Margaret Drive, Kelvinside, Glasgow
1936-9 Broadcasting House, Ormeau Avenue, Belfast
1936-9 Kirk of the Holy Rude, restoration, Stirling
1937 Annandale, alterations, Bearsden, Glasgow
1937 SMT Garage, Salkeld Street, Glasgow
1937 Nurses' Home, Royal Infirmary, Cathedral Square, Glasgow
1937 Grannochlie, alterations, Bridge of Weir
1937 St Nicholas Church, Hartlaw Crescent, Cardonald, Glasgow
1937-9 Ear Nose & Throat Hospital, Eldon Street, Greenock
1937-8 The New Locarno, Sauchiehall Street, Glasgow
1938-9 Almond Lodge, 4 Barnton Avenue West, Edinburgh
1938 Gilbert Bain Memorial Hospital, Lerwick, Sheffield
1938 Stands for RSAC, AA and Messrs Beatties Bakeries Ltd, Empire Exhibition, Bellahouston, Glasgow
1938 South African Pavilion, Empire Exhibition, Bellahouston, Glasgow (by George Miller) (reconstructed at ICI, Ardeer, as Africa House)
1938 Nairns Office Block, Kirkcaldy
1939 Calderwood Road, Newlands
1939 Killearn Emergency Hospital, Stirlingshire
1939 Killearn House, Killearn, Stirlingshire

Railway stations by Miller for which dates are not available:
Dalmuir Park, Eglinton Street, Inverkip, Roybridge, Tulloch, Tyndrum

Index

A
Adam, Matthew 38
Almond Lodge, Edinburgh 56
Anchor Line Building, St Vincent Pl 29, 30
Anchor Line Store, Yorkhill 35, 53
Anderson, Sir Robert Rowand 3, 21, 24
Ardlonish, Sutherland Ave, Pollokshields C2
Armitage, Joseph 43, 52

B
Balkissock House 54
Banks
  Commercial Bank, Bothwell St 50-2
  Commercial Bank, West Nile St 33, 45, 48-9
  Union Bank, St Vincent St 42-5, 47, 48, 49
Bayes, Gilbert 49, 52
Belfast City Hall 14-15
Belmont Parish Church, Hillhead 12
Bentinck Drive, Troon 16
Blanc, Hippolyte J iv
Boswell, George 6, 7, 29
Botanic Gardens Station 9-10, 21
Bournville
  Cocoa Block 45
  Dining Hall 44-5
Bridge St Station 8
Burn, William 39
Burnet iv, 1, 12, 43, 48
Burnet Boston Bell 7, 56

C
Caledonian Chambers, Union St 22, 28, 32
Caledonian Mansions, Great Western Road 10, 13
Caledonian Railway Company iv,3, 6, 8, 9,12, 13
Canniesburn Hospital 53-4
Carrick, James A 6
Central Station 8, 9, 20-1
Central Station Hotel, Hope St 21, 30
Civic Buildings
  Clydebank Municipal Buildings 14, 15-16
  Stirling County Buildings 54
  Troon Municipal Buildings and Concert Hall 16, 45, 46, 48
Clifford, H E 24
Clydebank Municipal Buildings 14, 15-16
J & P Coats Building, St Vincent St 49, 50
Commercial and industrial buildings
  Anchor Line Building, St Vincent Pl 29, 30
  Anchor Line Store, Yorkhill 35, 53
  Bournville: Cocoa Block and Dining Hall 44, 45
  Caledonian Chambers, Union St 22, 28, 32
  J & P Coats Buildings, St Vincent St 49, 50
  McLaren Warehouse, George Sq 37-8, 39, 45
  North British Locomotive Company Offices, Springburn 22, 30, 31-2
  Olympic House, Queen St/George Sq 28
  SMT Garage, Salkeld St 55
  Woodhouse Warehouse, Renfield St 47, 50
Commercial Bank of Scotland, Bothwell St 50-2
Commercial Bank of Scotland, West Nile St 33, 45, 48-9
Coupar Grange, Perthshire 15, 16
Craighuchty Ter, Aberfoyle 11-12
Cranston's Picture House and Tearoom, Renfield St 29, 34-5

D
Domestic buildings
  Almond Lodge, Edinburgh 56
  Ardlonish, Pollokshields C2
  Balkissock House 54
  Bentinck Drive, Troon 16
  Birkhall 53
  Caledonian Mansions, Great Western Rd iv, 10, 13
  Coupar Grange, Perthshire 15, 16
  Craighuchty Ter, Aberfoyle 11-12
  Dunloskin, Dumbreck 11
  3 Hillhead Gdns (19 Hillhead St) 6, 7,16
  Kildonan, Ayrshire 36-7, 41
  2 Lancaster Cres 18-19
  8-10 Lowther Ter 18-20, 22
  Newark Castle, Ayrshire 31
  Randolphfield, Stirling 6, 7, 39
Dunlop, Alexander 6
Dunloskin, Dumbreck 11

E
Ecclesiastical buildings
  Belmont Parish Church, Hillhead 12
  Kirk of the Holy Rude, Stirling 39, 50, 51
  Old West Kirk, Greenock 39
  St Andrew's East Church, Dennistoun 26
  St Mary's Episcopal Church, Aberfoyle 13
  Synagogue, Salisbury Rd, Edinburgh 47
Ednie, John 35
Educational and professional buildings
  Glasgow University: Materia Medica and Physiology Buildings 25
  Natural Philosophy Building 25, 26, 46
  Glasgow & West of Scotland College of Commerce 52, 53
  Institution of Civil Engineers, London 32, 33
  Institution of Mechanical Engineers, London 31, 33
  Lintwhite School, Bridge of Weir 16, 17
  Royal Scottish Automobile Club, Blythswood Sq 39, 40
  Wyggeston Grammar School for Boys, Leicester 46

F
Fort Matilda Station, Greenock 8
Forteviot, Perthshire 40-1
Forteviot Hall, Perthshire 40

G
Glasgow Empire Exhibition 1938 48, 55
  South Africa Pavilion 48, 55
Glasgow International Exhibition 1901 10, 11, 17, 18, 19, 33
Glasgow Royal Infirmary, Castle St 23-5, 28, 53
Glasgow and South Western Railway Company 8, 27
Glasgow University
  Materia Medica and Physiology Buildings 25
  Natural Philosophy Building 25, 26, 46
Glasgow & West of Scotland College of Commerce 52, 53
Gleneagles Hotel, Perthshire 38
Gleneagles Station, Perthshire 38
Gourock Pier Railway Station 8, 23
Graham, George 3, 8, 12
Gunn, Richard 6, 29, 37, 43, 48

H
Hamilton, David 42
Heiton, Andrew A iv, 6
Highlandman's Umbrella, Argyle Street 22
3 Hillhead Gdns (19 Hillhead St), Glasgow 6, 7, 16
Hodge, Albert 22, 33
Hospitals
  Canniesburn 53-4
  Glasgow Royal Infirmary 23-5, 28, 53
  Perth Royal Infirmary 33
  Royal Scottish National Institution, Larbert 52, 53
  Stirling Royal Infirmary 46-7
Hotels
  Central Station 21, 30
  Gleneagles 38
  Peebles Hydro 26-7, 30
  Turnberry 27-8, 30

I
Institution of Civil Engineers, Great George Street, London 32, 33
Institution of Mechanical Engineers, Birdcage Walk, London 31, 33

K
Kelvinbridge Station 9, 13
Kildonan, Barrhill, Ayrshire 4, 36-7, 41
Kirk of the Holy Rude, Stirling 39, 50, 51

L
2, Lancaster Cres 18-19
Lintwhite School, Bridge of Weir 16, 17
Lochhead, A G 42
London Midland and Scottish Railway 38
8-10, Lowther Ter, Great Western Road 18-20, 22
Lusitania 30-1
Lutyens, Sir Edwin 36, 37, 56

M
McLaren Warehouse, George Square 37-8, 39, 45
Manson, John Wellwood 56
Matheson, Donald 9, 12, 20, 21, 38
Miller, George 48, 55, 56
Mitchell, Sydney 19

N
Newark Castle, Ayrshire 31
Noad and Wallace 20
North British Locomotive Company Offices, Springburn 22, 30, 31-2

O
Old West Kirk, Greenock 39
Olympic House, Queen St/George Sq 28

P
Paterson, Oscar 21
Pearl Assurance Compay 1
Peebles Hydro Hotel 26-7, 30
Perth Royal Infirmary 33
Prince of Wales Museum, Bombay 31
Princes Pier, Greenock 8, 23
Princes Street House, Perth 42

R
Randolphfield, Stirling 6, 7, 39
Railway Stations
  Botanic Gardens 9-10, 21
  Bridge St 8
  Central 8, 9, 20-1
  Fort Matilda 8
  Gleneagles 38
  Gourock Pier 8, 23
  Kelvinbridge 9, 13
  Princes Pier 8, 23
  St Enoch Sq Subway 9, 10, 12, 13
  Troon 8
  Wemyss Bay iv, 6, 9, 21, 22-3, 26, C2, C4
  West Kilbride 8, 9
  West Highland 9
Richmond Memorial Hall, Kirkoswald 40, 41
Royal Scottish Automobile Club, Blythswood Sq 39, 40
Royal Scottish National Institution, Larbert 52, 53

S
SMT George, Salkeld St 55
St Andrew's East Church, Dennistoun 26
St Andrew's Halls, Glasgow 42
St Enoch Sq Subway Station 9, 10, 12, 13
St Mary's Episcopal Church, Aberfoyle 13
Savoy Music Hall, Hope St 34
Sellars, James 42, 56
Sims, Charles 33
Smith, George 39
Stirling County Buildings 54
Stirling Royal Infirmary 46-7
Synagogue, Salisbury Road, Edinburgh 47

T
Tait, Thomas 42, 48, 53
Thomas, Brumwell 15
Thomson, James 1, 2
Troon Municipal Buildings and Concert Hall 16, 45, 46, 48
Troon Station 8
Turnberry Hotel, Ayrshire 4, 27-8, 30

U
Union Bank of Scotland, St Vincent St 42-5, 47, 48, 49

W
Walker, Sir Alexander 16
Walker, James 6
Wallace, Captain David Euan 36
Wemyss Bay Station iv, 6, 9, 21, 22-3, 26, C2, C4
West Highland Railway 9
West Kilbride Station 8, 9
Whyte, Robert 30
Woodhouse Warehouse, Renfield St 47, 50
Wyggeston Grammar School for Boys, Leicester 46